The Poetry of the Dust

Michael Briggs

Acknowledgements

Like most apologies, I'll start with the argument. When I first started writing this collection, publishing was my last thought, mainly it was a way of stretching my soul a little. With the encouragement of my girlfriend at the time, I began taking it seriously and started trying to decide what, if anything, I was trying to say.

As for the poems themselves, I knew that I wanted to mix styles, to explore the idea of what a poem could be, and to inject as much anarchy into as I could. Poetry is now and always will be an act of protest, an act of rebellion against an uncaring Universe. I wanted this collection to reflect that as much as I could, whether or not I succeeded, is up to you dear reader.

At the beginning of this, I said there would be an apology. This is it. When you try to write good, hopefully great, poetry, there's a level of pretension and self-awareness of that pretension that's required to do it. And so, I apologize for any act of hubris that you find along the way, my only excuse is it had to be there.

Acknowledgements are so many it's hard to list them all, so I'll stick with the major ones. My mother and my father obviously, both played such a huge impact on my life that I wouldn't be who I am without them. And I thank them now for their always unceasing love and support.

My maternal grandmother, now passed, who showed me what it truly meant to pay with a pound of flesh. Both my brothers, my steadfast companions and biggest supporters, without whom none of this would've been possible. Lastly, to Joanna Money, who gave me back the courage to try and the heart to do it with.

EGYPT

The loss of a child is humanity's first true experience with loss. It is our oldest sadness, and our most profound. It's the loss of the future, the loss of hope, a broken heart and a broken soul.

It is timeless, and has followed us across the broken track of our existence as a species on this planet. That's why this first section starts in Egypt, a man mourning the loss of his child.

This is the first era.

-The Poetry of the Dust-

A seed, a hope

A glimpse of the past and future become one

A dream left undreamed

A denial of chaos redeemed

The whisper of a daughter or son

A dark bit of laughter

From on high in the rafters

The Universe watched with yellow eyes

"You're a fool to hope, but here is some rope

And for now, I'll say my goodbyes"

A blink of Shadow

The hush of new fallen snow

Then it was gone

A rush of emptiness

Cradling grief to my chest

As I listened to the whisper of the wind's song

I watered the Earth with my tears

And buried with it the hope of my remaining years

Then let happiness die on the vine

This is the poetry of the dust

Of how all things end, as they must

And of the bittersweet vintage of time

-The First Kingdom-

Slaves of the moment

Never suspect such a thing

As the future

Houris amongst the fields

Never suspect such a thing

As consequence

Reality requires context

The truth demands its point of view

Neither relies on fact

The gold flecked sky

Tinged with bronze

Caps the world

The silver hued desert

Shaded with rose

Rolls away to the horizon

The Pyramids at Dawn White limestone gleaming

Cast long shadows of judgment

Here there be monsters

Fed by ice

Succored with moonlight

Full moons are empty tombs

Cold stone coffins

Lined with silken misplaced guilt

There is no perfection

This side of death

Only moments of tranquility

Moments the universe pauses

Graces you with love

The love of another and of yourself

From my bed on the sand

I contemplate Eternity And the horizon

The roll of the dunes

Mirroring the contours of her hips and thighs

-The Middle Kingdom-

The wind punched holes in the clouds

Windows for the voyeuristic

Moon to peek through

I'm broken and tired and bruised

There comes a point if only loneliness is consumed

That your body screams for the touch of another

No matter who they are

Every primal chord in our life's song craving another's embrace

There is nothing left but ash and dust

Coating our tongues and the words they form

You are the light in my heart's darkness

The breath in my soul's lungs

But life is carefully manicured

Chaos Masquerading as Order and moves

To its own demands, follows its own rhythm

A song unto itself

A symphony even our genes must join and follow

And I can feel you slipping away

Lost to the undertow

-The New Dynasty-

Languid waves lap

Against the sides of the barge

Whispering ancient secrets

The verdant shoreline

Is alive in the moonlight

Predator and prey moving in humid need

The barge puts in

At ancient Karnak

The nightingale's song greeting us I walked amongst its columns

Mingled with its shadows

Then through, to the desert beyond

The sand had begun to chill

But a breeze off the River Still carried warmth

Alone, atop a dune

I surveyed the deserts Moonlight beauty, and wept

A zephyr rose

Stirring a dusting of sand

A baptism and a balm Consecrating me

In the Holiness of Solitude

-Hathor-

The Spring clouds tumble in

Behemoths Clothed in joy

I'm listening for the Echo of Eternity

Listening for the Song of Stone

To the Rivers whispers amongst

The sawgrass and reeds

GREECE

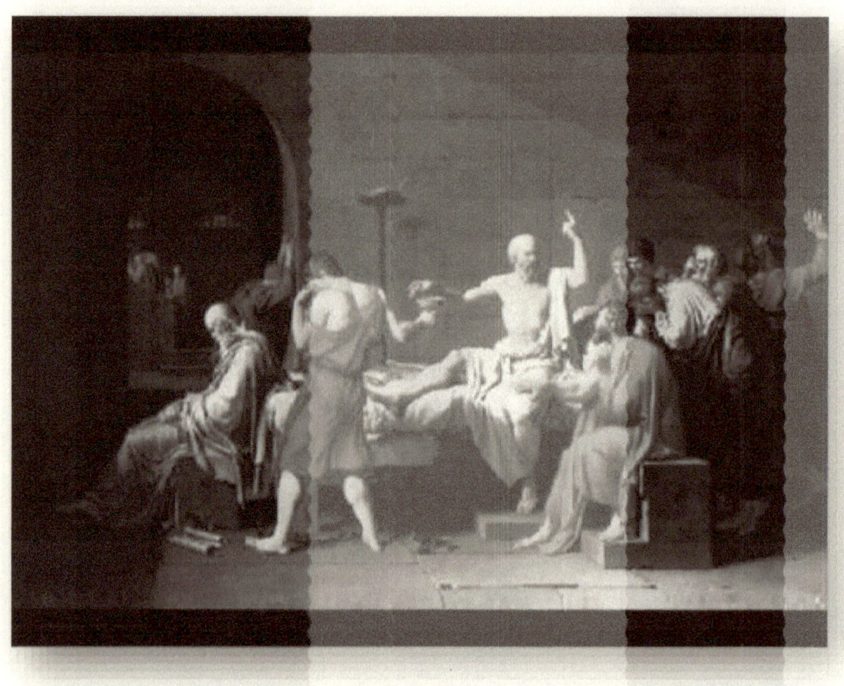

One of the earliest books I can remember picking up as a kid still learning how to read was a copy of Edith Hamilton's Mythology: Timeless Talels of Gods and Heroes, something which sparked my imagination like nothing else I'd read to that point had.

This led to both The Illiad and The Odyssey later in my teens along with my first introductions to The Republic and the great early Western philosophers.

Hence, this section begins first with poems of the philosophers and then the heroes. Poetic liberties have been taken with nothing but love for the source material.

This is the second era.

- Diogenes-

The difference between dreams and scars is often as slim as hope and regret

A single candles flame awakens the bedouins soul

I'm a ghost

I can feel my heart rattle I can taste your approach

Slip Drip

Glide on by a pantomime

For the Passerby

I feel the xenophobia In your hug

Feel the hunger In your eyes

The brittle porcelain snap

Of a promise unkept Misdirection is tradition

Deny Lie

Shade the truth a bit

All the morals

Of an alley cat In heat

The Season is a prison Voices whisper

Let loose the linchpin 'The center cannot hold' 'Things fall apart'

Why shouldn't you?

But I refuse to play hopscotch With the voices

And tighten all the nuts and bolts Holding my sanity together

The Feather of Ma'at Is heavy

-Plato-

I can feel the Night staring Drunk on its own darkness and waiting
to pounce

I deny it

And embrace the stars caress

There's a savage beauty in their gaze

The opalescent regard

Of the long dead millennia

Piercing Nights long black veil

Diamonds, sapphires, and rubies

Anoint the Moon ascendant

With vibrant cobalt sparks across that ebon shawl

I feel hope stir

A forgotten guest but welcome nonetheless

Spreading its wings wide in my chest

A cascading majesty

Born of the Universe's secret

Love is an energy that never dies

Only varies between potential and kinetic

And even as the stars shine on long after their Suns have burnt out

So does the energy of love live on

Long after the lovers are dead

I hold my arms wide, embracing the Stars

There is a savage joy in their gaze

And I revel in their regard

-Epicurus-

The Land remembers

Under a waterfalls Hidden spray

I touch the sandstone

I feel it all around me

The Earth is Alive with memories

Its heartbeat never wavering

A life is both Water and Stone The shaper and the Shaped

There's a pulse, the Heart of Creation Older than Time

A Well of Knowledge Deeper than the centuries

I hear a rhythm

A song, a chant of Life

Embraced by the ardent stars overhead

I long to dance with you under the starlight, the bonfire bright

The Moon is high! The bonfire bright!

A throbbing cinder of the Sun, fallen to Earth

Come, grab thy drum my love, and beat a rhythm

In time with your heart

We'll dance, naked as the Dawn

Round this Primordial Flame

Satyr after Nymph

Until Exhausted, we fall into that most precious embrace

Alive in each other's eyes

Souls bound under starlit skies The Land remembers

It whispers

Can you hear it?

-Diomedes-

Hardest work I've ever done

Was working on the farm

Easiest work I've ever done

Was holding you in my arms

We seek safety in the remains and of the day

But the shades of the past Get in the way

Goddess, grant me a glance

A second chance

Lace

Soft and fragile

The spider webs from which

Lust is woven

Filters the afternoon sunshine Into shadow and fleur de lis

There is a stranger

Between my legs

Enthusiastic

And trying to impress me

So why does this stir nostalgia And not my own excitement? Her
hair is red

An ember cast out of Heaven And into my lap

She burns

Her lust an open flame

Incandescent and warm

A balm against the late afternoon October antumbra

She looks up

Eyes shining

Her body rising behind her

Until

With serpentine grace

Her hips meet mine

Hallelujah

A busty purple

And burlesque orange

Bleed together as the day fades away

I spent the day without regret

Without trying to unbury the past

Without trying to find words to unsay

I'm no Don Quixote

I know who's beside me

There are no lies in her eyes

Only adoration and supplication

Greet me

The cloud dance across the Sky

Embers driven by the setting Sun

Listening for a whisper

An echo lost in the whirlwind Just ghosts

Lost in the gaps in Time I try to sift a meaning

From the ashes of the day

I remain haunted by the moments

Between here and now

By the ash of yesterday

A night wind precedes the Moon

Dreams of Eternity stir

Drawing close

A lovers embrace

Memories pile up

Storm clouds beyond the horizon

Empty promise and hubris

Behind the wind comes the Stars

Winking shy promises

Whispering

Let the past die

-Menelaus-

-I- Before the Flood

My mind races

Paces

Stalks around the room

My thoughts are performers

Mourner's

Contemplating their own doom

If you're going to be gored anyway

You may as well take the bull by the horns

Sophistry never saved anyone

Is it masturbation

This hesitation?

A pointless itch to scratch?

Hungry for the future

We're eating the ash of the past

Secret joys and pains

Other lovers

And other names

There is no now

Only the endless snowfields

Of the Waiting

Where every second contains the death of centuries

-II- The Deluge

My mendicant heart

Pleads for your holy embrace

An almsman begging

For your love

What's the point of sleeping

If you have no dreams?

Pilgrim soul, your every movement is art

Let us take our time, no need for haste

Just the moment, nothing less nor more

As Eternal as the Sky above

Slowly, slowly, January molasses creeping

Immersed in a love which redeems

But the Passerby stands apart

The graveyard of continents in their gaze

Esoteric knowledge beyond what we adore

No olive branches, no white dove

Only a sundering rift, ever deepening

Every diamond is flawed, no matter how it gleams

-III- The Alluvial Plain

I stir

Murmur

The Cambrian cracking around me

The dust and mud

Of an Epoch

Falling away to a whisper

Placed upon the freshening

Eastern wind

The Unknown

Has shown its teeth

Vanity

Pride

Arrogance all lay beneath

I rise to my knees

Still whispering pleas

Supplications against the dark beast

Here on the Alluvial Plains

All has been laid bare

Washed away in Fury

And only those strong enough to love remain

-Odysseus-

-I- Solstice

The river fog lifted its head to ponder

A morning fog pouring down off hills

Then reached out its hands to embrace it

Brother, it said, come take my hands

We are the same you and I

The world is silent

The air is still

Take my hand and we can trade our secrets

Whisper our fears

And clothe this world in mystery

But the hill fog only shyly slid by

Thinning and pulling back

As the day slowly warmed

Under a caramel-colored Sun rising in the East

The dryers whisper in the background

And a family of woodchucks sample

Dew covered grass as that caramel hue

Bathes the world in its first blush

There's an ecstasy in the morning

A clean and pure virtue

That screams for lust

In our joy, we ran beneath the Sun

Careless of consequence

Mad with our love

Only to find we had outrun the horizon

I feel like a phantom in the rain

A man with no shadow

Or past

That Sun now shines through me

Offering neither grace nor balm

And I wonder whether a Soul

Can wither through Indifference

My love comes to me

I think of the river fog

Then hug her tighter

My fears turn over in their beds

Then settle

Quiescent and sated

My soul cries to hers

The coyote singing to the moon

A call as old as life

Later, when the afternoons shadows Had grown thin and narrow

She raised her head from my arm Gently kissed my forehead

And whispered prophecy

Ancient words set to the rhythm of my heart

Then seared them on my naked soul

With a kiss upon my lips

-II- Equinox

A sympathetic orange blushes in the East

Blooming against a low cloud bank

The birds begin to dive for their morning feast

While the Moon, sated, slowly sank

I've been watching the river foam dance

The morning fog nestling against my shoulder

I stand on the railroad bridge, immune to chance

Staring down into the fog and dark water roiling below and a fate
much colder

It would be so easy

A step

The fall

An end

Peace

The Sky opens and begins to weep

As my sorrow finally begins to sleep

The Dawn wind drives it into my face

I turn my back on the bridge, and return to the world looking for my
place

It's been a long night in conversation

With the passerby in my soul

I toss two coins into the River as compensation

And wonder if it will buy my way past the toll

Past the bridge maples spring toward the Sky

Turning the tracks into a Cathedral

The orange light through the fog and mist of rain dazzle's my eye

And my heart is suddenly full

There is still magic in the Universe

There is still mystery, still wonders

I think of her words, both prophecy and curse

I feel the ties Time will never sunder

The morning fog is heavy as it rolls through

Heavy as the tide that pulls you under

Lives little more than sunbeams made iridescent with dew

Leaves dancing in the wind to a clap of thunder

But they are never meaningless

Whether they be empty or full of wonder

Whether there are more days behind than in front of us

We walk the trail that life has set

But never meet a day with regret

Remember all those you've loved that you met

And that we've all already paid Charon's debt

-III- The Tempest

Sandpipers flee down a deserted beach

The horizon lay offshore, just out of reach

And bruised thunderheads rolled in from the West From my
dunetop, I surveyed Eternity

While the tide slowly took it away from me

The moment broken with each waves crest

Weakened times reflected in the evenings magenta tones

The sand beneath my feet held the secrets of our bones

Even for the dead there is no rest

From behind layered clouds firefly pulses of arc lightning cried
aloud

Embrace even those you detest

For even this shall pass

Denied, the Past whistled through the sawgrass

And I counted myself blessed

I walked to the shoreline to gather the hope I'd missed

And to release every choice I'd ever second guessed

Then turned my eyes back to the West

I embraced the storm on the horizon

And the one in my breast that rages on

So that I may finally rule the Tempest

For there is no Sea of Woe

Nor any future we've yet to know

That will matter more than that conquest
The first of the rains walked me home
And I let my heart roam
Having finally put my pain to rest

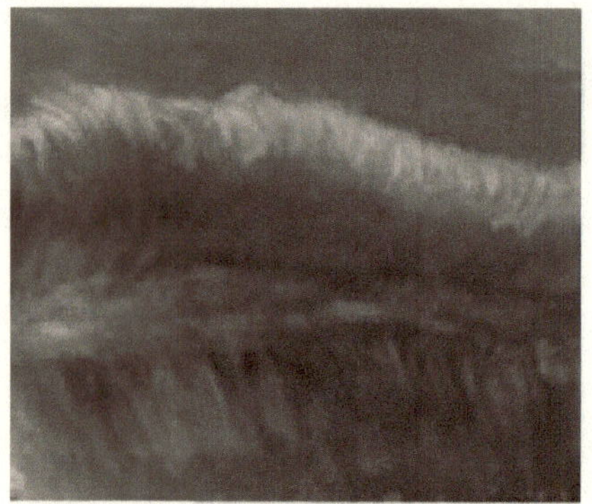

SAINTS

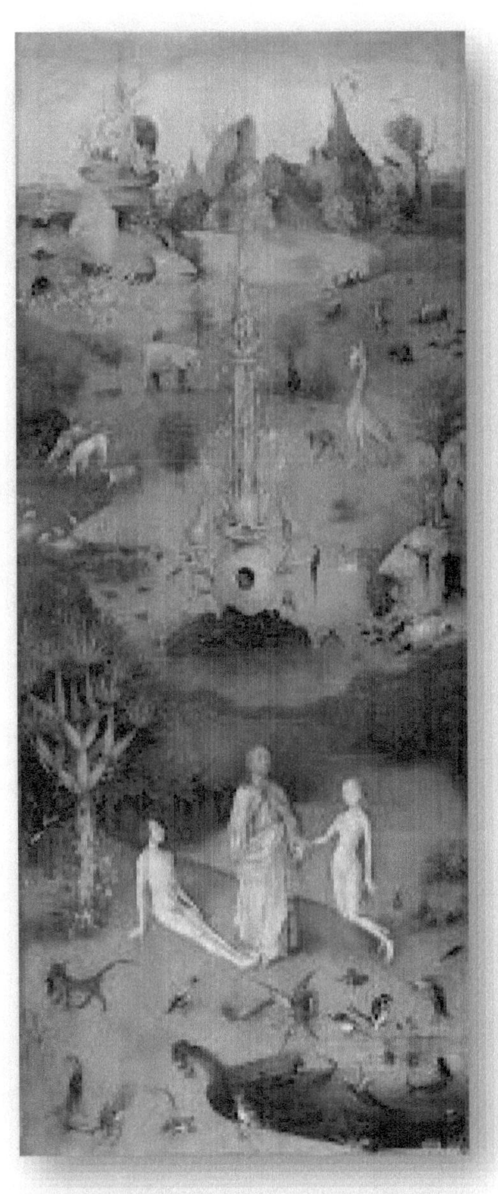

While not a Christian, or even an agnostic, I still have always had a fascination with the stories in the Bible and the lives of Saints. There's practical advice and a pretty good set of moral guidelines there if you need them, and Jesus tossing the moneylenders out of Temple will always strike a chord with me.

This section either invokes the named saint in some way (St. Simeon=saint of fools, St. Barbara=math) or is taken from the Bible. This is the third era.

-Saint Simeon-

Two old men argue

Shaking balled fists on the lawn

One wears a red cap, the other a shirt of blue

Same old argument, same old song

One pecks his head like a chicken

Spitting vitriol with every verb

While the other deflects again and again

And counters with expensive words

I'm waiting to see if it'll come to fisticuffs

Or if their geriatric rage will fizzle

Blue's wife pulls at him, violence is beneath us!

Red's wife aims him like a missile

The argument is over a parking spot

But the stakes have obviously been raised

Each is an example of the kettle and the pot

And each wants their color praised

There's a storm on the wind

Dark clouds piling upon the horizon

Waiting to see if the fight will begin

Spectators before the wind carries them on

Red pushes blue and blue flips him the bird

They grab each other and wrestle around

Abstract meets the absurd

Red's hip breaking when he hits the ground

Both have lost a bit of their dignity

A little bit of their Ego Self

I call 911, tell the operator a little bit about me

Then make a date later to put my elf on her shelf

A Life is a strange thing

Random moments strung together

A chain of pearls defining our Conscious Being

A series of decisions as fickle as the weather

Beauty formed from something annoying

Now an old man is writhing on the ground in pain

And I'm going to get a blowjob after I date her

Both our sins will be washed away in the rain

And I'll light a candle for Saint Simeon later.

-Saint Thomas-

I've had a recurring dream

Of Saint Thomas passing Me by

The street is narrow and filled with fog

A yellowing haze that nuzzles my ankles

Swirls amidst my thighs

Then lays clinging about my shoulders

With all the tenderness of a jilted lover

I know I'm here for a reason

But the currents in the fog distract me

With me whispers of decadence

And sugarplum girls

He appeared suddenly

Melting from the shadow

And tripping over a loose cobble

A burning candle from an open window

Colored the Saint in the colors of Samhain

Oranges and yellow and blacks

Play over his robes in a kaleidoscope array

A murder of crows takes flight

Swirling the fog in eddies of mixed emotion

He straightened his robes and rubbed his tonsure

Looked me up and down

Then gave a nod, his bald pate gleaming

What's in a nod?

Scorn? Disdain? Acceptance?

An acknowledgement of culpability? All that and more?

'I heard you were a thinker'

I replied I tried and occasionally succeeded

He cocked an eyebrow and displayed a tapestry Filled with a
lifetime of choice

And said 'then what do you call this?'

I shrugged it off, said we all make mistakes

You can't even decide where you want to be buried

He was forced to concede my point

Though it was at the tip of a sword 'what are you hoping to
accomplish?'

He asked quizzically

Again, gesturing to the tapestry

'All this running around and fucking?'

Not all of us are blessed With immaculate celibacy

In response he turned his eyes towards the Father

A beatific smile on his face

And his heels rose six inches off the ground 'Can you do that?'

He asked slowly settling back on his feet I scratched my head

And allowed that was a good trick

But not as good

As two girls on your dick

'The Lord gave you a brain for a reason'

The Mind observes but the Body preserves

'Domine, conserva nos'

'Puer stultus est'

I asked him

Why are you arm wrestling for my soul? What gaineth thy Lord

By my preservation?

'Your brain boy'

He replied, and a terrible darkness

Began to form between the ramparts Of his scowling eyes

Purple thunderclouds

Scarlet lightning riven Through his irises

'It's not living, it's merely existing

'To never know the touch of love 'Only the embrace of lust.

'Love involves your brain

'Frees your heart

'And completes your Soul

'God gave you a brain to find your fucking soul'

I'm struck dumb

Literally and figuratively

He steps forward and I fight the urge to retreat I can feel heat baking
off him

A fire that radiated from the inside out

His eyes are no longer his own

His voice is no longer his own His words

No longer his own

'Pono tibi cerebrum Et cor tuum supra Mentula causa'

He placed his hand upon My shoulders

I can feel the power in them

A buzzing of ozone crackling Around his brow

'Vita te praeterit

Te decernere oportet Quis es Quod vis

Et qui vis ut faciam tibi'

He shoves me and my body Is a feather in a hurricane

The yellow fog swallows me His last words chasing me

'Her name is music on your ears Her love the blood in your veins

And you know she feels the same Wake up boy

Exsuscito!'

I awake screaming

Blood pounding and heart racing

Yelling I'd already found her

She's lost and I'm broken

A sweat covered bed my only solace

He's right of course

And the dream haunts me

Both prophecy and curse

Nothing born of love is every truly lost

Merely misplaced until

The pound of flesh re grows

And we can once more bear the cost

-Saint Dominic-

I can hear the voices

Of every heart I ever broke

Crying in the stiff North wind

The fire crackles at my feet Knot's popping occasionally

The wind awoke me

Its plaintive wails piercing my doze

I wait for a sense of guilt

A pang of conscience

A whisper of heartache

But only felt old I'm getting used

To being a mushroom

At least it's peaceful It's entirely possible To do everything right
And still fail

I stir and it sends needles Through my hip

Reminding again of my pain 'Welcome to the monkey house'

It hurts when it first arrives

But you become immune to it

Until it reminds you

A letter from an old friend

That gives you a paper cut

When you open the envelope

I stare out the lone window

A bay now covered in hoar frost

Watching the ice crystals dance

The crescent phase of the Hunters Moon Winks from behind a curtain of clouds

Balefully taking my measure

I place my dreams upon the dog star

My eyes locked now on it

Bathing in its arctic light

I can feel it calling me home

-St. Barbara-

What is the geometry of happiness? The circumference of
fulfillment?

Do right angles complete us

Or only box us in?

Does a circle comfort us

Or only leave us chasing our tails? Whether obtuse or isosceles

The triangle makes an uncomfortable point

Can you provide x from y and z?

Show your work

Use your math mind

Think outside the box

Remember your constant

For Time and variable for Chaos

As represented by your revolutions

Around the Sun and the current State of your heart

What is the sum of your life?

Take the quotient

Of how many times

You've danced in the rain

And the days alone

Staring out a window

At that same rain

Find the hidden value

Of x by multiplying that number

By the number of moments

In the sun, hands clasped

Eyes locked and two hearts made one

By dreams fulfilled

By seconds bathed in children's laughter

There are any number of formulae

To give life its balance

To measure its purpose

But the sum of your life is not happiness

Happiness is fleeting

A warm breeze on a Summer day

The sum of your life is the love that you felt

And the joy you've experienced

These are what you carry with you

Into the last days of your life

These are your lights

Against the coming of the dark

-Saint Paul-

People react

Like paranoid Androids

The prosthetic extension In their hand

Is alive with Its own demands

Letting it do

All they're thinking

A dream within a dream

While never sleeping

Alive only by existing

In a haze

Of constant outrage

It's not about

What they've earned

It's about

What they're owed

'There But for The Grace of God Go I'

Is lost on them

It's not about faith

Or God

Or the dust

Or You

It's about recognizing Your life's moments

In the Sun

It's about humility

And being grateful

For what you do have

The joys you've earned

And the falls you've

Picked yourself up from

You never fail

Until you give up

But

To self-made pariahs Humility will never

Earn them your sympathy

Better to feel

You're owed the privileges

You claim to hate

Within every rebel

Is a closet aristocrat

As Robespierre so aptly taught

It's not about equality

It's about the need to punish

And no matter the flag

You drape yourself in

No matter the letter

You voted for at the ballot box

No matter the political philosophy

You wear like the Emperor's New Clothes

That's fascism

It's a fascism of the soul

Of the mind

And of the heart

So,

There, but for The grace of God,

Go I,

An atheist

For there is a beauty In language

That makes it holy

No matter the denomination

Which spouted it

And I am grateful for my joys

My scars

My tears

I am grateful

For every dance in the rain

Every kiss in the moonlight

Every hug from a child

Every second lost

In my love's eyes

But this is something

A thinking machine cannot understand

A soul built on outrage

Cannot understand true sympathy

A heart built on avarice

Can never truly give And a mind built

On the need to punish

Will never allow free will

So,

There, but for

The grace of God

Go I

Against the fading of the light

For those drunk on time

Appreciating the moment is a crime

When they still feel they're

Owed the future

When I'm gone

Not even my dust

Will be a memory

And I'm grateful for that as well

-Leviticus-

Long ago

In the time before time

There was an idea

What if kindness could solve the world's problems?

Then the Buddha shat up his soul

And fed us his Karma

And Andy Warhol

And Nikki Minaj

And the pretensions of soulless Twats

Do unto others

Has no effect on masochists

While the eternal Tao Fades before indifference

Pop culture has swallowed

The Muses souls and gave

Us nothing but recycled ideas

And pretension mistaken for cleverness

There is only one dream, one certainty

There's still nothing new under the Sun

-Timshel-

The Devil showed up one day

Talking shit

So I bent Him over

And fucked His tight little ass

For a Fallen Angel

He made a lot noise

But the ball gag solved that

The world is what we make it

And sometimes the best way

To deal with all the barking beasts

The World places before us

Is to feast on the flesh of our enemies

There's waves to this journey

The Ocean of Life is broad

And deep

And treacherous

And wonderful

So when Old Nick shows up

Pitchfork in hand

And evil in His heart

Remember Timshel

And the promise of Hope!

AROUND TOWNE

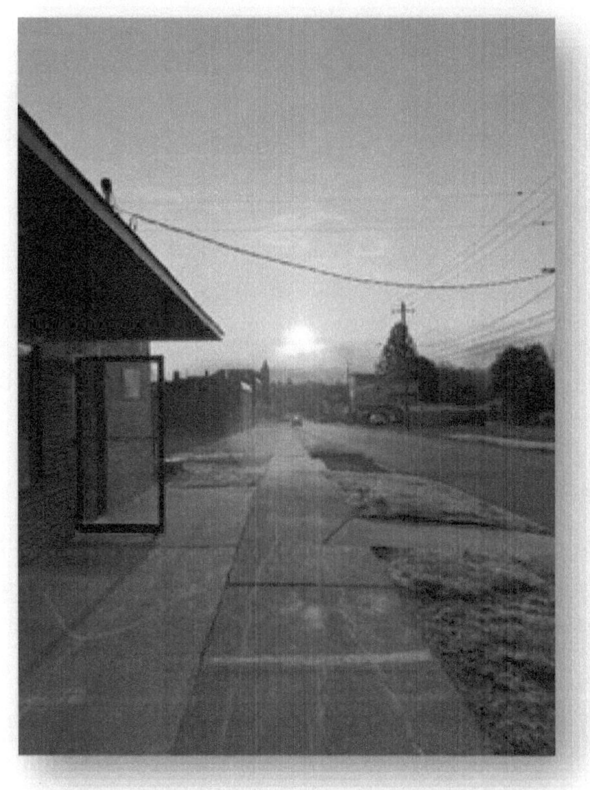

My family has lived in the same small town in upstate New York since 1815, give or take. That is, at the time of publishing, 110 years. That is not as long as some, but it's more than most in this area, and a large portion of that has been in my particular patriarchal branch, dairy farming.

Dairy farming is obviously quite heavy on the milk aspect, but there's also a lot of other stuff that goes along with it, picking stone for fields, growing corn, making hay for the winter months. My point is that over the course of that time, there is going to be a lot of your blood, sweat, tears and, eventually, bodies being put in the ground.

Those are roots that it's hard to define because they aren't just the haze of rose-colored glasses for where you spent your childhood, those are roots that become grafted into your DNA, and you can't ever really escape those.

This particular section of this work is entirely set in my hometown and experiences I had there growing up.

This is the fourth era.

-Fever-

(for my mother)

I came to my mother once

As a child a nightmare had woken me

She told me go back to sleep sweetheart

Monsters aren't real

I told her I didn't think that was true

Even then I knew

There are monsters in this world

Through our demons given form

She rose, and took me by the hand

And there was comfort from her white night shirt

Where it brushed against my cheek

We went back down the hallway

The late hour casting shadows

Filled with Dread and chill

She whispered reassuring words

To brace against the alien corridor

And asked what I'd been dreaming

Purple explodes across the sky

I told her

There's thunder and rain

And I'm alone in the mud I call out for you

But my voice is not my own

My thoughts are not own

You pass me by, never looking down

On your way to somewhere I've never been

Nor will ever be

We reach my room, the bed clothed in shadow

She picks me up, tucks me back in

I can feel her looking at me for a moment

'There's nothing to be scared of'

'It's just a bad dream'

Everything terrible that's ever happened

Was just somebody's bad dream

Waiting to be given form

That's how demons are born

I can tell she's troubled, but my mind is addled

She murmurs something

A balm?

A question?

I can't tell, the shadows on my ceiling are dancing

Round and round and round

Circles then triangles then circles again I barely feel her lips on my forehead Her worried hand on my brow

Or the sudden call for help

Consciousness is a slender rope

I feel my grip slip

And then there was only the darkness

In the cedars

Round and round and round

Circles then triangles then circles again

The shadows dance

For three days they dance

There's white silence

Without and within

I climb Jacob's ladder to consciousness

And I'm in a hospital bed

My mother's hand in mine

No matter where I am

No matter how I feel

No matter what I'm doing

I can still feel her hand in mine

Pulling me up out of the mud.

-The Bridge -

I woke to a melancholy grey day

Looking for the words to say

There's got to be a better way

As I walked away

Our love the dust beneath my feet

And where the past and my shadow meet

Sifting through words that had no deceit

I looked for a way for our souls to meet

As the day warmed and the Sun shone through

The birds began to call and the Sky turned to blue

I looked for words to bridge the gap between what we say and what we do

Only to find the bridge had fallen through

And as I walked away

I found there was no better way

I found there were no words to say

Only the ghosts of yesterday.

-The school-

There's an old brick building just down the street

You can tell it used to be nice

A beautiful facade that catches every eye it meets

And stucco the color of newly formed ice

The cornerstone bears the date 1927 A stately and august year

A Solstice moon sits overhead

The streetlights wink out, one by one

As the Dawn creeps over the hilltops I'm alone in the chill steel grey light

The subzero temperature hushing the world

Staring at a date

And trying to imagine the world then

It's hopes and it's dreams

It's trials and it's tribulations

And the secret joys held close to its heart

The world has moved on

And those hearts with it

Passing to rumor and myth

History and Fates interlocked

Dreams and aspirations dust in the wind

A century in the dirt, mud, and shit

Of humanities collective consciousness

Led to me

Alone

Under a solstice moon

A light dusting of snow on my shoulders

And a question on my lips

Where did all the yesterday's go?

Are dreams Eternal, do they have an end?

Or do they just pass on to the next generation

Like sins or blessings we carry

Birthmarks against the dying of the light

I've no answers

Only more dreams to add to the midden

-A Morning by the River-

In the early morning, I went down to the river

To clothe myself in memory as I sat and shivered

Cradling the ghosts of conversations long passed, I remember a shoreline fire

As I sat down beside her

And we spoke in tones of prophecy

Who we were going to be

What we were going to see

Of the long roads we saw before us

But she only played Cassandra

And I merely a poor Nostradamus

While we lost all our moments

To the river that flowed beside us Slowly, so slowly, she mounted me

We flowed with the river blissfully

Behind us the bacchanal raged on

The night slowly wound toward Dawn

While the river fog embraced our steaming bodies

I felt the agony/ecstasy of release

I felt her soul break beneath me and we gave ourselves to Eternity

I can still smell the smoke

Hear the words we spoke

And the feelings we awoke

In the lifetime since that morning by the river

Our dreams lost their vigor

Our hearts grew no bigger

The truth of them contained in a simple shiver

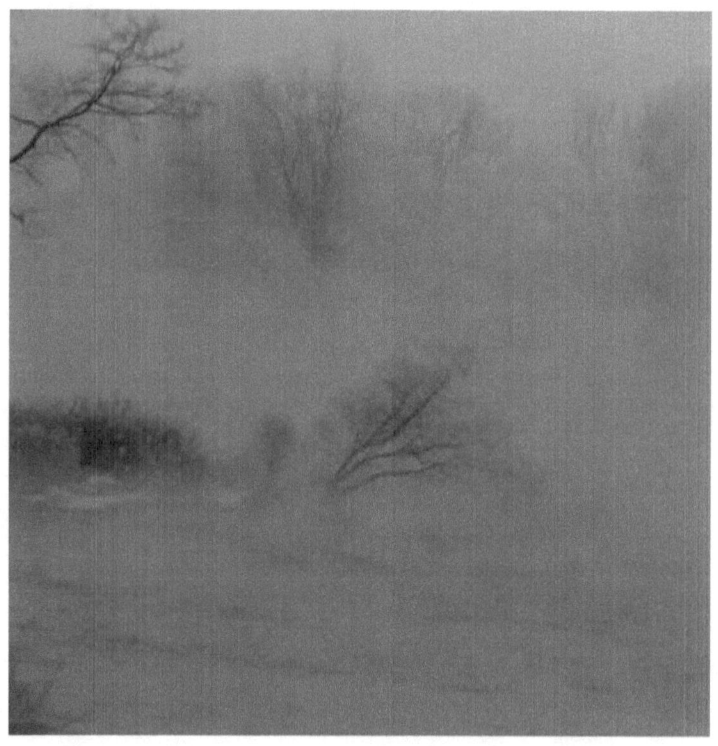

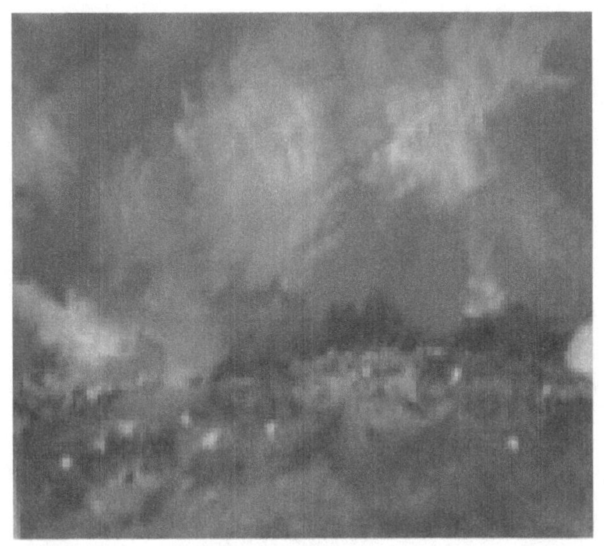

-The Field-

I long for the ecstasy

Of her head between my legs

And the warm touch of her hands

Upon my chest

Trailing fire with her fingertips

A lovers caress

Wrap me in the scarlet of daybreak

In the softer shades of mid morn'

Lay me down in a field of heather

And bathe my face in tears of joy

Goldenrod tips it's head lazily

Nodding it's approval of our love

The fog rising off the lake

Wraps us in its embrace

The memory of dreams scented

With the ghosts of all our yesterdays

Sleep my love, my life

Find succor in dreams

Take paths untraveled

And drift with the clouds

Across the cerulean Sky

Fall into my arms once more

So we can exist in each other's breath

And feel our love expand beyond

Our hearts and Time's fragile demands

-The Bus Stop-

There's a Karen in my face

Or maybe it's a Terry

They haven't identified their pronoun yet

There was a certain lividity

To their whiteness

A shield they wore around them

All reality

Exists within a spectrum

And they hit everyone that could find

Their shirt says 'Eat the Rich'

And I can tell indignation is always in reach

It was their privilege to be offended

To be the protector

Of those they deemed inferior

Their voice is not as loud as their hair

Though it is a close second

There's a sort of blackened

Cynicism in their protection

An assumption of victimhood

Positive stereotypes

Still murder

The individual soul

I feel like pointing out

You can't be both kind

And condescending Oh shit…

They're cursing me

So I must've said it out loud

It feels like the Light of Reason

Is being put out

Like the world is slipping backwards

Into a bunch of howling monkeys

Looking for a longer stick

To beat each other with

This all started

Because she thought bums

Stole her iPhone

And she was trying to compel

It's return with cash and the

Assurance she could empathize 'if I were some rich asshole

'I could understand 'but I'm a good person'

The bums seemed unimpressed

Melancholic at best

Surly at worst

So I thought I should add in

Before a real argument

Could begin for they/them

'Lady, you've had an iPhone

And got driven here

In a Tesla, to them You're the rich asshole'

I saw two derelict nods

A sly chuckle from a third

Then they moved on

Leaving me at the tender mercy

Of an offended upper middle Class White Knight

And a bus driver behind schedule

-The Wind-

There's a big wind on the hill tonight

A brash Cyclopean rampage across the sky

There's a sorrow in it

Bitter as the North

And it's touch will chill you to your soul

Her eyes feel the same

Wild and sad and lost

Laugh at adversity

She said to me

And press your lips to mine

For a time let us ease our minds

And take what joy we may

From the grim and frigid night

There are tigers tails in this world

Disguised as kindness

There are cycles to life

And rhythms to it's pain

In between search for meaning

Amongst the silence

Hands and lips and tongues

All the familiar vices

Our eyes bind us to this moment

Touch and taste and scent

It all falls away

Until there is only cold and the wind Howling its loss

-The Storm-

A Spring Rain

Fresh and clean and without pain

Came across the horizons girth

And it's voice carried rebirth

The heavy scent of the Earth

And it's chatter off rooftops was a refrain

A baptism in the sussaration of thunder

South came a zephyr to clear the clouds asunder

A spring sun peeked shyly upon the life beneath

Gentle and loving with life to bequeath

A rainbow appeared as a wreath

And the life reached toward it in wonder

The last of the storm blew away

To where the hinterlands held sway

The world felt fresh and born anew

Clean and pure as the Sky's cerulean blue

Fresh and new as the morning dew

And full of the promise of yesterday

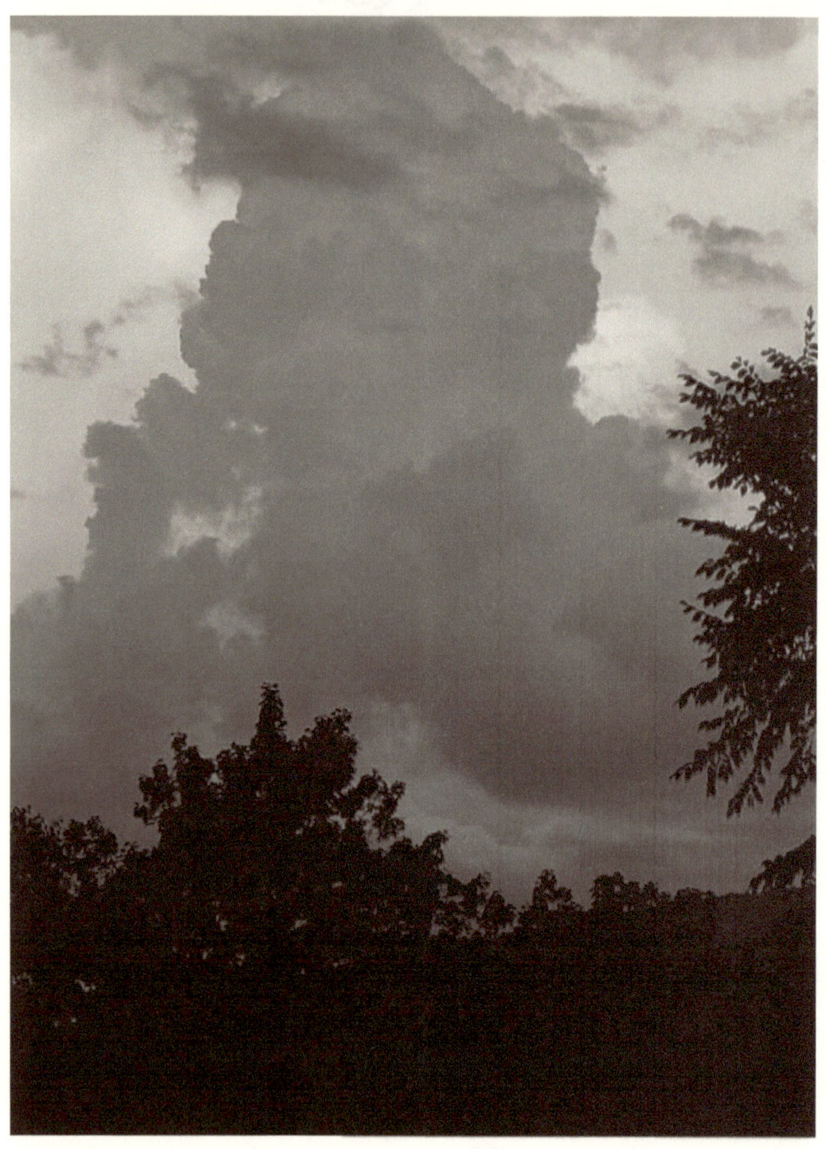

-Wildflowers-

Awaken my soul with your kiss

Unseal my heart with a look from your eyes

Change my outcome

With limbs outstretched

Imagine a love

And all that comes next

Bend thy stem toward me

Turn your face toward the Sun

Bathe thy petals in the dew

Of our passionate embrace

-Storia-

'Boy! Won't this take you back!'

There were circles under his eyes

Whether from lack of sleep

Or fear of shadow people

It was hard to tell

What's that?

'Remember your senior year girlfriend?'

Emily Sue? Hard to forget her

A cherubic dew drop

Dimpled and curly haired

Eyes twin chips of azure

The mere glimpse of which

Stirred one to poetry and song

Whatever happened to her?

'She's got six kids and is the size of a bus'

No shit? How'd that happen?

'She got pregnant six times'

Obviously. Wasn't she valedictorian?

He pointed to his own eyes

His own teeth

And his own heart

I nodded, and shook my head

There are no words.

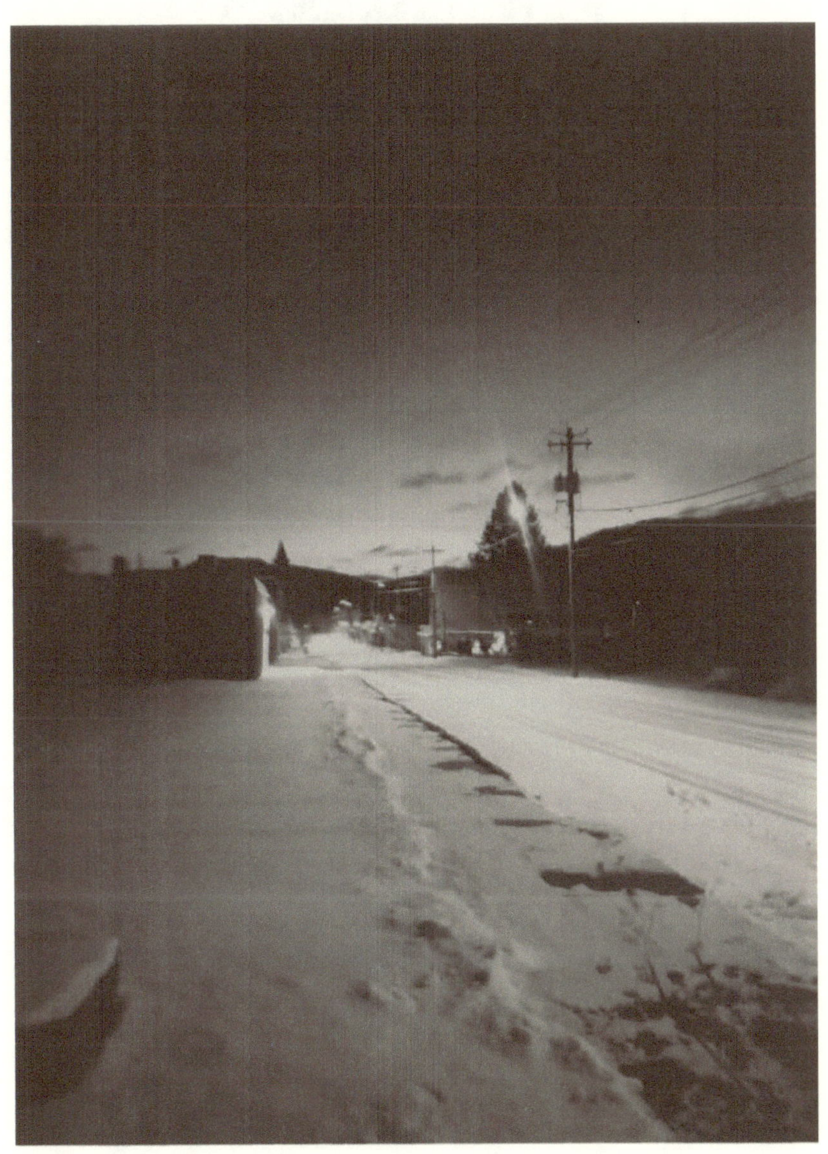

NEW ORLEANS

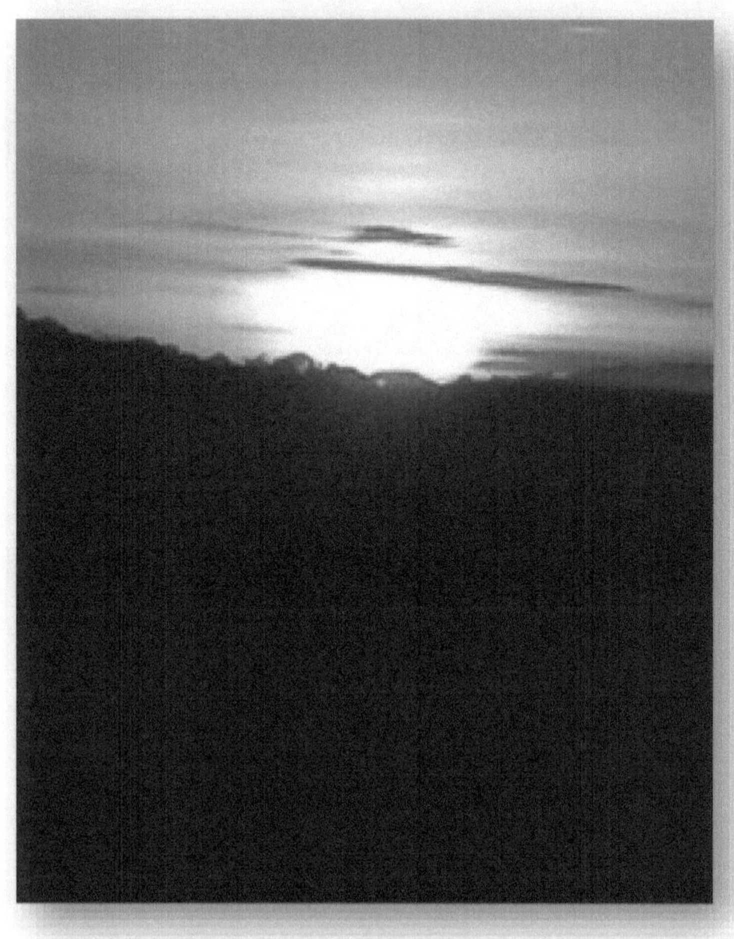

I moved to New Orleans from my hometown when I was 21 and I was enchanted from the moment my train crossed over Lake Pontchartrain at sunset, lighting the entire horizon ablaze with hope and passion.

I moved there because of my girlfriend at the time, and when she met me at the station. I lit her up with that first kiss. While that is a terrible reason to move to any place, it ended up being one the best mistakes of my life, one I treasure to this day, and this section is dedicated to some of my memories there.

I'm going to date myself a little bit by saying this was New Orleans before Katrina, so it is a Crescent City that truly exists only in the collective memory.

This is fifth era.

-Sublime-

She strode from the room

A golden brown Aphrodite dressed only in streetlights and shadow

Fleeing under a Crescent moon

Gone like the whisper of smoke or a lingering scent upon ruffled
pillow

Morning grey filled the room

And carried her final words across the diamond expanse

'Adios, Space Cowboy'

-Dreams of Byzantium-

Fleeting and cloying decadence

Passion as sustenance

Humid kisses with dancing tongues

Pants and bra undone

Sexual collision was the mission

Identities lost in juxtaposition

We felt our Souls undone

Then danced all night to the song our bodies sung

An early morning fog begged along the Rue'

As we made one out of two

We kept our love on the run

Chasing the ghosts of the previous millennium

The morning passed quickly

The afternoon warmed thickly

And we embraced dreams of Byzantium

Under a Summer Sun

-Poor Rambler-

I'm restless

Caught between nothingness

And Everything

I want to cavort, my limbs akimbo

Joints unlocked and flailing

Against the ludicrous

I want to lay down and sleep

To fall into the cracks between Eternity

And be swallowed by the face of Time

Where is tomorrow?

What was today?

How did yesterday get us here?

Who are we now?

When did the moon occlude our hearts?

I'm restless and tripping over questions

Voiced and unvoiced The past falls in place With a click

The future remains out Of sync, ineffable

There's a horizon waiting for us

An oasis amongst the palm and date trees

A dream under a rock

A thousand years of thought

Silenced by the hush

Of centuries of indifference

By the ghosts of words without consequence

And by Dawn's first blush

Venus treasure me

This rare blush I see

In your eyes are the lightning sparks of lust

-Thaumaturgy-

Every night I die

Between your holy thighs

I fall further into your dreams

Lust in tension

With chastity

A dying star

Extinguished by the Ocean of Night

A moon

Falling toward ecstasy

Falling toward release

Falling toward illusory peace

Silver occluded by onyx

She straddles me

Mourning her lost Youth and agility

You'd never know it

By the hungry way her hips meet mine

A denial of the dust and ash

There is rebirth on her lips

Falling with the Moon

Falling with her eyes on mine

Falling with her musk leading the way

Ebony and Ivory

Moving in perfect Synchronicity

Lost in the Eternal Tao

Each breath a lifetime

Every movement a symphony

Our pleasure a revolt

Against Eros' approach

Falling towards sleep

Falling towards whatever tomorrow awaits

Falling toward the Dawn

There is coffee in the morning

Gentle conversation and scrambled eggs

Stolen caresses and shy glances

She borrows a book

Ezra Pound's Personæ

As a promise of tomorrow

I run my hands through her hair one more time

Thick and full and strong

Then she is falling

Falling back to further shores and shadow

And I'm praying for the next Moon

-Magazine Street-

She had eyes the color of sin

And a voice of black satin

This Queen of Magazine Street

That arrived on the wings of a Storm

And a mind that would not conform

Filled with the spider webs of deceit

Her body hit you like a Summer day

But you always felt lucky when she looked away

Lest you grovel at her feet

Her skin was the colour of darkest night

Hair that moved between caramel and umber depending on the light

And dazzled every eye it did meet

An Afro piled high and framing aquiline features

Holier than a million preachers

Promising both the trick and the treat

I want to use her

To fill her

To amuse her

To thrill her

But never love her

-Rue de Chartres-

The clouds moved on and revealed a star field

A gibbous moon sat ascendant

It's pale eye a slim crescent

And under it's malevolent gaze

I quailed

It danced along the horizon

Before it ducked behind another curtain

Of steel gray zeppelins

Occluding the night sky

And I felt as though a curtain had been thrown over the world

And the passerby within me stirred, and murmured for release

The world was moving on, and I was alone

At the mercy of memory

Drowning under the weight of dreams

I was alone

I closed my eyes against the undulating waves of the hills

Closed my ears against the cry of the loon

Closed my soul against the burden of Self

And closed my heart to the pull of companionship

There's a freedom in Apathy

A bounty even when in the midst of a Barmecidal Feast

There's a holiness in loneliness

Yet even the most callused heart can bleed

The deepest sleep can withhold dreams

And the truest smile mask despair

There is succor in madness

But no release in violence

No mystery but the one behind the

Grey curtains drawn behind

Steel grey zeppelins

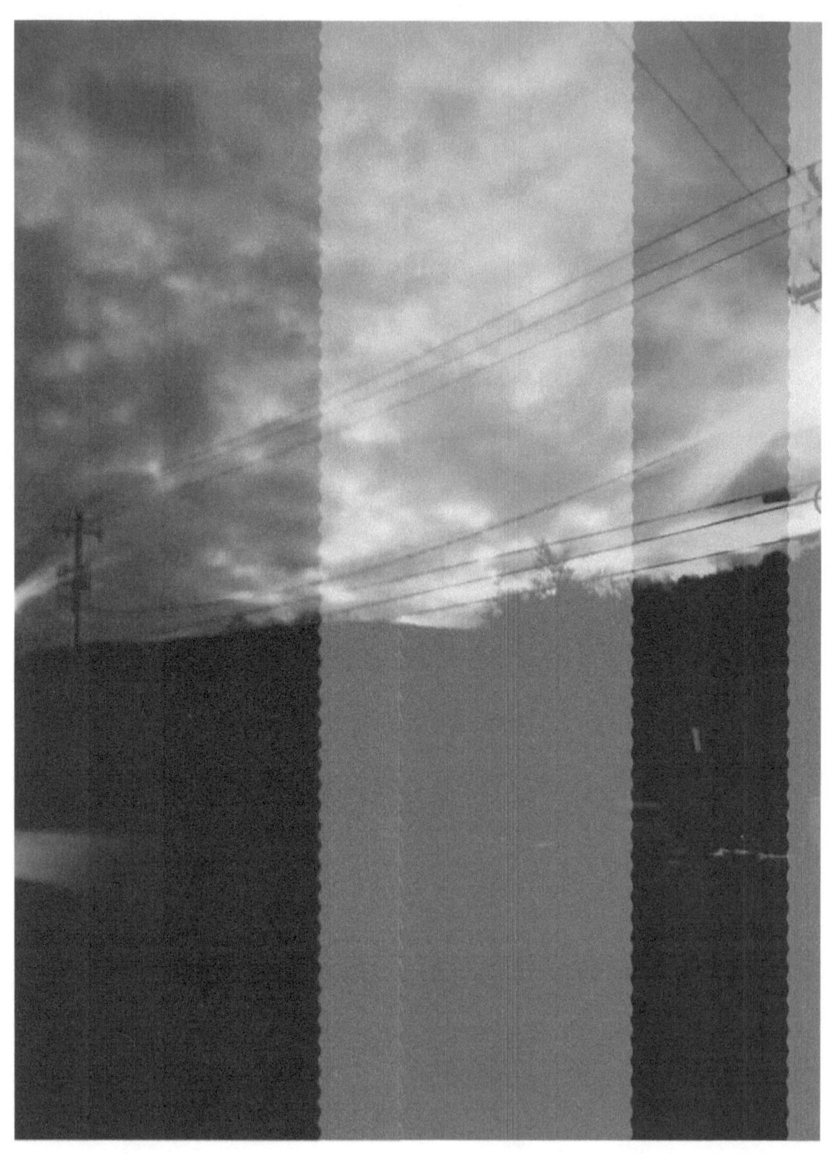

-Jackson Square-

The ferry stirs up oil slicks

In the river, creating little whirlpools

Of iridescent pinwheels in its wake

A mother and child are near the bow

She's wearing an orange sundress

A cute red ribbon holding her hair back

Back straight and proud

She leans down and points across the river

The boy is holding her hand

Serenely eating cotton candy

Eyes on the further shore

A Saints jersey on under his Oshkosh

I'm struck by them, my very genes

Responding to the pair, for there

Is power there, a power to move Nations and change the World

A young mother and her son

On a ship, her one arm pointing

Toward the further shore

Promising him the horizon

I turn away

Shaded by my own cynicism

Losing myself in the mysteries

The pinwheels shape in

The dark Mississippi water

When the ferry arrives, I head For Jackson Square

It's 4 in the afternoon and

The tourist trade was in full swing

The air humid, pungent with

Open containers and hops

I took a seat near the cathedral

Idly people watching and smoking a joint

I didn't notice the priest at first

So intent was I on the tableau before me

The hissing shuffle of the decks

The sibilant whisper of the crowd

The narrowing futures before me

When he spoke, a polite request to

Share the joint, I jolted, sure the future

Was whispering to me

I was a bit taken back

Expecting an attack rather than camaradiere

He replied that if my eyes Had seen what he'd seen

Heard what his ears had heard I'd take a toke as well

I handed him the joint and lit

Another of my own, smoking in silence

When he'd finished he clipped it

Offering the roach, but I waved him off

Telling him to keep it for harder times

He smiled and gave me a

Blessing

I spied the mother and son and asked

They received it instead

The future belongs to mothers and sons

Not half baked Poets lazing about Under an August sun

-Rue Decatur-

Music pours out in the street

Shaking hands with passers-by

Winking at pretty girls

A blonde sauntered by

With hips like a hearse

And a personality to match

She'd be willing to let you take a ride

But it would be to your grave

The streetlights burned bright

Sodium suns illuminating the night

The blonde cast an imperious eye

The music quailed and trembled

Eager with lust and entropic with joy

An optimistic puppy at her feet

She disdained to notice

Swaying her hips into a fog

That was quickly swallowing the Rue

The music, now chastened and subdued

Slunk back into the club, disconsolate

And rested its weary head upon the bar

I order another gin and tonic

The glass is sweaty with condensation

Or maybe it's my eyes

Leaking quinine and regrets

The night passes into the Witching hour I meander out into the fog

Piss drunk and half blind

Then wobble left up the street

It's not long before I run into the blonde again

Sashaying her way back down Decatur

I paused, and met her eyes with my own

She met them unapologetically, curiously

Honeysuckle and jasmine

The first touches of a June rain

A caress by Autumnal wind

All swept over me and I was staggered

'Didnt I see you earlier?' she asked

I stumbled an answer

Something about passers-by

And chance encounters from a barstool

She laughed, and eyed me anew

'You lonely handsome?'

Ah! The secret joys of early morning

Later, when she was dressing

I wasn't hurt when she asked for Benjamin

All life is a transaction of some sort

Even love must have a commerce

As I drifted off to sleep

I pretended not to notice as she lifted my watch

All life has consequences

Why shouldn't love?

Three humid days later

I was watching street drummers

The steady rhythm keeping time with a slight rain

Every downstroke a wave of sound and water

The Sun, falling in oblique shadows

Cast stick figures dancing behind the drummers I caught a glint of
gold

Then saw my watch on one of their wrists

Life is a circle

Why shouldn't love be?

OBSERVATIONS

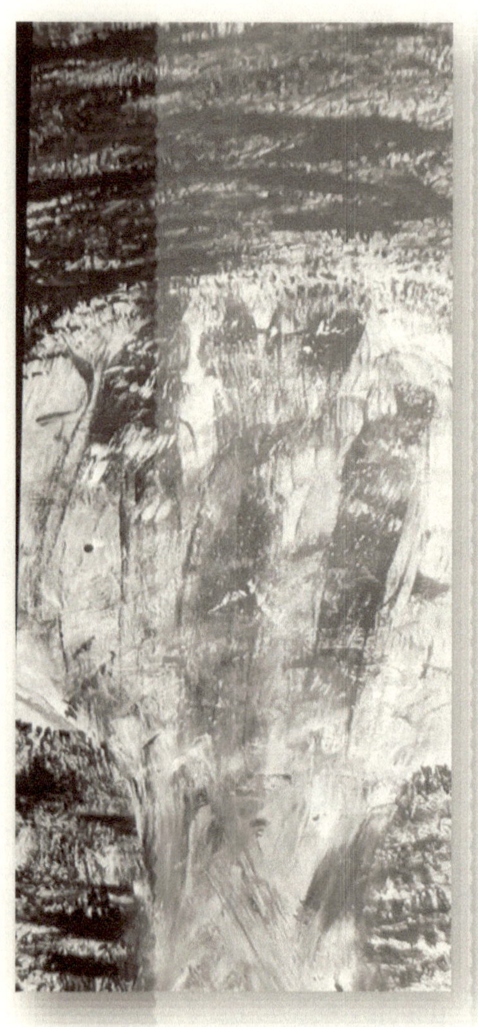

America has been kind of been devolving into hysteria and an ever-increasing cynicism ever since Barack Obama left office in 2016 this section is devoted to a lot of the things that I've noticed happening along the way, both personal observations on my own life and how the nation has been going.

This is the sixth era.

-The Mask-

Wear a scowl as protection
No one approaches a sour puss
Especially if they're single, white, and over 40
Isolate before rejection
They can't turn you down
If you were never available
What is touch?
A concept
A memory strained through fog
Be a man
Die at work
And get buried at the job site
A nightingale sings in defiance of the dark
A sweet call against the coming night
A thing of beauty set before the fear of the unknown
I'm alone
Dressed in shadows
But the mask is in place
A single molecule
Hiding under the petticoats of circumstance
Is there a dream, an oath, a prayer
That might lighten the shadows
And hide these aching bones
From the ghosts of Twilight

-Thy Brother-

Words scamper

Emotions clammer

Yet only the Wise may be struck dumb

The future doesn't matter

When you're Mad as a Hatter

Drunk on the Moon and your brain a drum

Thistle and burr collect random thoughts

Bark and skin display battles fought

The years leave their mark until you're numb

In the mud there's no time for the Sky

No time for happinesses lie

The only songs your bloods constant hum

Who we are in the shadows

Only our secret heart knows

Intentions laid bare in charcoal and plum

You can't change a life with good intentions

Or lift someone up with lowered expectations

In trying to hide where the emotions and words came from

When there is blood on the ground

All the evidence has been found

We created our own ghosts and they haunt all our days to come

It's often the self-inflicted wounds that don't heal

The deepest emotions we fail to feel

Never recognizing the synergy between the voyeur and the bum

-Carry On-

A grackle alighted upon a limb

And cast a weighted eye a'dim Upon my troubled brow

I asked it for the time of day

But an opinion it would not say

Upon the passage of the Now

I asked for an opinion

Of whether to begin again

But it would not answer how

I asked for its advice on the goings of the night

In response it took flight

With a parting trust in the Tao

I gave a shrug of my shoulder

And tried not to smolder

Just watched cotton candy dirigibles as the day took its final bow

I made my mind a clean slate

And found a way to wait

Until I found a way to carry on

-The Bad Guy-

Forcing another person

To be who you want them to be

Rather than who they were meant to be

Is the most perverted type of coercion

There's an arrogance involved

Hubris, self-love, and unchecked ego

Combining to turn someone into your shadow

The lines between abused and abuser dissolve

Sacrificing another's life

To the altar of your own strife

It's your hands that hold the knife

It's your Gods price for the afterlife

And your hands to set the bridges a'light

Their disgrace your delight

So long as you keep them below you

There's an arrogance

In thinking you're doing God's work

A vessel filled with equal measures Messiah and Martyr complex

You've no concept of either

Isaac or Iphigenia Only your own shadow

Filling your soul

We're never the villain In our story

Before we would remove

The speck from our bothers eye

We ought to look to our own

-Cascade-

The dawn slept in, and let the birds begin their songs without it

The first of its winds carried the heavy damp of an incoming storm

But the horizon promised only skeletal stratus clouds

Slowly Aurora shuffled in from the East

Her robes trailing red, oranges, purple, and pink that set the ridge
line ablaze

As the first light swept down the river and across the hills and rock
quarry

I could feel the world open one eye and ask for 15 more minutes

My dreams instruct me in parables

I sift that wisdom and measure it against Infinity

While Dawn slowly spread it's mantle before my still dreaming eyes

There's a family of swallows in a hanging basket on my porch

I think we've made friends, but it's hard to tell with a bird

They're just so flighty

Slowly, the great ball of fire crested and the swallows woke

And a'lighted to find their morning meal

Lord, save us from well wishers and good intentions

My soul is dried up rice paper

Dusty and ready to crumple under a strong breeze I walk down

Front Street towards the river

Following a path cut by a peculiar cumulonimbus

Lake people drive by, off to do Lake People things

Pick blueberries or drive-up housing prices

Hollow people with head pieces stuffed with straw

Frail dreams held up with future plans

Always the horizon, never the ground they tread

The water flows deep and black and calm

Eddy's drawing the silt and driftwood to them

Like old spinsters collecting rumors

We measure ourselves against past participles

I wished

I hoped

I tried

Defining ourselves by past actions rather than future choices

I feel empathy leaking into the river from my eyes

We can till the land and harvest the fruit

We can bleed for the crop and water the ground with our blood and
tears

We can bury the dead and try to forget

But we can never own the land, though it may own us

Even as our bones become the wood and stone of the Valley

Time hides its face amongst the reeds

While the Moon lays its heart to rest

-Paralytic-

The beginning of knowledge

If that's the path you'll follow

Is the awareness of what you don't know

There can be no wisdom without that

I love people who look to the Night Sky

And wonder, Why?

Who seek amongst the Stars

Peer into the Infinite

With an inquisitive eye

Their mind is alive

Curiosity their drive

In the most human way possible

Searching the mystic for the truth

And finding the meaning behind a meteor shower

The need to make corners square

And Life a circle

The problem began

During the span

Of the time we learned to cross

The emptiness of space with images

There was a time

When people would find

They're measure against those around them

Their neighbors, and kin, and such

Then came those from afar

Now people measure against the stars

And refuse to look in the muck and the mire

For the porcelain vase

Longing to be released by their hands

The bread and circuses have won out

And there's little doubt

We're moving backwards

Away from each other

Towards a cliff

A yawning abyss

Never realizing how dangerous

This loss of the human connection

Will be for everything that follows

The need to make corners a square

Life a circle

And our existence a journey

Rather than simply a destination

-Sawyer Street-

There's a little Portuguese man

Following me up the street

We passed each other half

A block up, saffron, clove

And linguica leaking from a corner butcher shop into the

Turgid September afternoon

He did a doubletake as we Crossed paths, a queer look

That made me look back

He trailed me, eyes locked On the horizon beyond me

His hair was parted sharply to

The right, a hatchet for a nose

That broke sharply left, his face

Was a contradiction

Lips the colour of liver worked

In a mumble I couldn't hear

I'd been chasing my own shadow Much of the morning

Trying to find a why

Never knowing I needed a when

My Northern European-ness sticks out here

Like the little fellows glasses perched

Upon that broken nose

The genetics of the whaling boom

Still run strong here

The city is old and cloistered in its way

A microcosm and orgasm crafted together

In a distinctly early American way

The cobbles and narrow streets of Old Town whisper the secrets of
centuries

Sotto voce in the morning shadows

The old man appears to be both Avatar and antithesis personified

Gregarious in their old age

And ancient with youth

I stop, curious what this secrets this

Hoary and wistful gnome

Had pried from the wind and fallen leaves

Of life and days gone by

Would it be Browning's Hoary Old Cripple?

Yeats Old Pensioner?

Eliot's bearer of Staves?

He shambled up and whispered in

A voice crafted by Pall Malls and

The surge of tide over the ship's prow

'Your flies open kid'

Sometimes we forget the best wisdom

Is sometimes also the most practical

-The Mantlepiece-

Go dance in the raindrops

Cavort beneath the Moon

And seek respite amongst the fog

There's a stillness at Dawn

A calm in the air

Broken only by words

Consonants and verbs linger

Whispers in the breeze

The clouds flee from the North

Zeppelins filled with lightning

Desperate to leave their anger behind

There's a charge in the air

An energy born of emotion

Pheromones burning through

Imbuing the æther with purpose

Dust motes dance in the sunlight

An updraft lending them ecstasy

Counter clockwise gyres

Before they slip upon the breeze

And saunter away

I want to live in this moment

Preserve it in amber against decay

And place it on a mantle for all to admire

The sunshine had a weight

A physical presence to it's embrace

I welcomed it

A lost friend

With it came a sense a

Peace A welcome shawl

And pleasant a smile

To close the fade of the day

-The Dandelion Seed-

Memories float by without focus

Dandelion seeds on the breeze

Washed out memories

Of someone else's black and white photos

The evening Sun felt thin

While the shadows stretched into misplaced nostalgia

Framing the fleeing clouds into archways for Valhalla

And I can smell the rain coming again

Oh to be a dandelion seed

Born on a Summer storms wind

Weightless and free of sin

A being born of shapeless need

To wander from place to place

A dream on a zephyr

A wish for something better

And thereby attain Grace

Before returning to the Earth

Putting down roots

And putting forth shoots

To begin the cycle of rebirth

-Gypsy-

What does it profit someone

To always be

First person possessive?

I, me, mine

Never we, us, ours

Lord knows there isn't

Enough time in the day

To say

Another life exists

Outside your own

Let alone acknowledge

Sin is only expunged

And hubris overcome

When you take responsibility

For the harm you've done

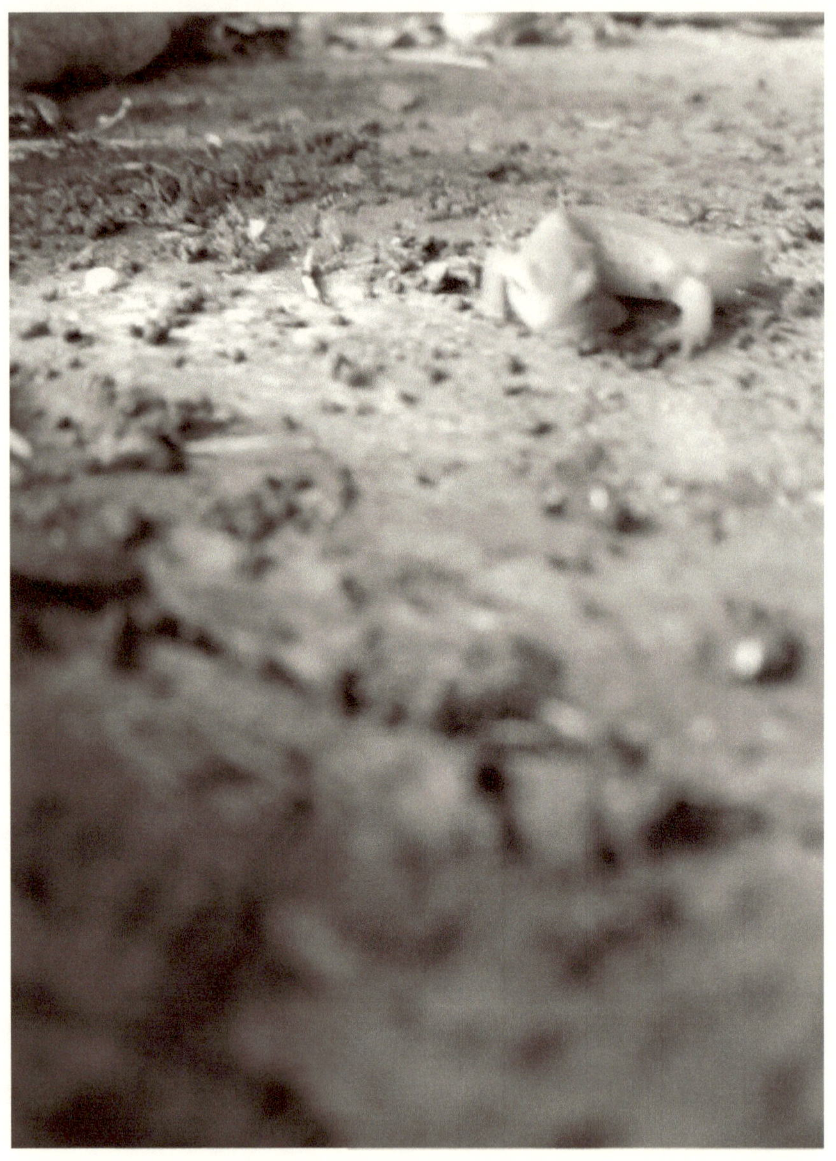

CONSEQUENCES

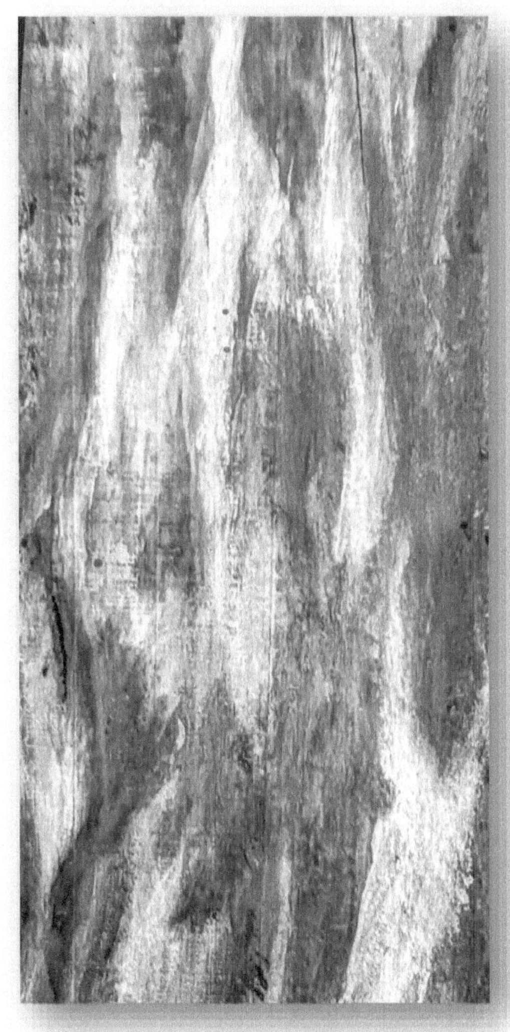

*All of life is filled with decisions, moments where we pick the person
we want to be. These moments are always filled with the
consequences of those decisions, and we always bear the
responsibilities associated with the cost of that decision.*

*This section is devoted to those moments, moments when the cost of
my decisions was extracted from me.*

This is the seventh era.

-Memory-

As I had a mid-morning smoke

And tried to shake the mood with which I'd awoke

A mother Cardinal and her chick landed upon a limb

The chick was a drop of toffee and yellow needing a rest from the
wind

Beating its tiny wings rapidly to loosen muscles not used to the
stroke

And I fought the memories it awoke

The mother stood near

A honey hued dream watching all she held dear

Slowly recover from the flights strain

And learns that life is pain

Sparing quick glances round in case danger should appear

The sky was a creamy pale blue

A singular cumulonimbus sailed through

My mind drifted to folklore

And a wish for something more

A vibrant pulse of red streaks past my vision

And the father joins his family, taking a sentry position

While the mother moved closer to encourage the chick

And the moment clicked

My eyes teared

The sorrow became clear

Oh my son

-Divination-

If you saw my face through a diner window

Would you come in

And give me sweet release

Then give me a thousand days more?

Or would you turn, uncertainly

And turn up your collar to disappear

Into the late afternoon crowd

And flee into the Sea of Humanity?

-Reserve-

Caught between apathy and rage

Whether to delay

Or turn the page

To simply obey

Words will fade

Actions be undone

The feelings cascade

Yet, I'm still the lucky one?

Memories ghost

Are tears in the rain

Phantom boasts

Just another way to hide the pain

Our love fell in on itself

An abandoned building left to

Time Rotted timbers and toppled shelves

Mildewed corners hiding the crime

Was it a moment, a touch, a thought?

The shackles of apathy

Or the bonds distance wrought? I've no eyes to see

No anguish or anger over the battles we fought

It's reserve you sense in me

There was never a more

Divine time

I ever devised that compared to your eyes

Bright, clear as stars on a bitter winter night

Shining, twin suns granting me new life

But from a box it's hard to see those eyes

Feel that embrace

To hear I love you

So I lock my heart away

Bury it in shadow and stardust

Deeper than the passion can reach

Deeper than any lesson can teach

-3 am-

Words fall in perfect cadence

A rhythm as old as time

Disguised prophecies

Always fall on deaf ears

I'll die upon this hill

Built on the bones of Time

Buried by the Past

The moment never works

I chased the dawn

Eager and filled with hope

Cradling secret thoughts

I sought the Darkness

When you place a whisper upon the night wind

Be prepared to treat with what answers

The push of the Dawn wind

Came up from the river

Affirmations and curses combined

I felt no lighter, no seven ounces shy

But remain haunted by those amber eyes

And a voice of empty night

Days passed to years

To decades

To a life

Until one chill midwinter's evening

Alone

Cold

Bereft in my bed and weary of life

There came a scratch upon my window

Hesitant and eager

I could feel a wanton need

Leaking through the curtains

A mewling lust absent of any blush

No thoughts were in my head

Only a chill dread creeping under the covers

Caressing my ankles

My calves

My thighs

A formless need

Resting its head upon my chest 'Is this death? Is this peace?'

My thirty pieces of silver

Long since spent

I still owe a pound of flesh

The consequence

Of a soul valued too lightly

Now a cold, lonely death was due I have it willingly

Glad to be free

Ephemeral body shed

I ride the night winds now

And cry after those

Lost as I had been

Eager now for Abaddon's embrace

-Daybreak-

Rage, red rage

Burns the night sky

I want to bathe the world in napalm

Gather the dust and nuke it

Then salt whatever is left

To bind mine enemies to the rack

And to bring their line to ruin

To punish the wicked

And vilify the pure

Then drown those that remain in blood

To be a comet igniting the velvet dark

Before bringing desolation in my wake

To be the tsunami racing across the ocean face

Before drowning the land in my grief

To be the earthquake rending the Earth

Before swallowing light and joy and happiness

In my darkness

Both the volcanoes eruption

And the pyroclastic cloud running down the mountainside

Choking all memory of hope from the world

There's a violence in silence

That remains unvoiced

There are narcissism and hubris both in Rage

Tinder before the spark

Eager for the flame

Wicked in their needs

They whisper of cosmic anger

They urge unrelenting violence Inflame minor slights

And enrage calm men

To terrible deeds

I finally lay my head down to rest

Rage, red rage

Burns the Dawn sky

Filling my dreamy eyes

With the dance of flame Filling my dreaming ears

With sermons of hate And I fall

Into darkness

Released at last into the æther Of Morpheus' embrace

Free from the Harpies

Of self hate and the chaste

To chase the memories of

Elysium round until the first blush Of radiant dawn gnaws at my

Dreaming mind

Grey, pristine grey Haunts the day

Depression dresses like an old lover

Cloying grey robes

And soft grey eyes

Willing arms and limbs

Draw me in again

Better the disconnect than

Stiff necked rage eating

Away the joy in my day
A sickly yellow Sun climbs
Over the horizon with apology in its limp
The sky turns mustard gas grey under it
Towering storm clouds pile upon each other
Across the Southern horizon
Lightening dancing like houris amongst its
Uppermost reaches
There's an electricity in this mercury heavy day
A holiness in this moment teetering between
Self ruin and self hate
Between rage and depression

-Juno-

I hide in silence
There can come to be
An arrogance in repentance
Hubris in an act of contrition
A sin can become
A source of pride
A conversation starter
It forces one to wonder
Whether it's the joy of confession

Or the thrill of shock

Which drives the urge to share

Beware the Jabberwock

And self-made Pariahs

The difference between a hypocrite

And a hypochondriac

Is three degrees of separation

So avoid the temptation

To self aggrandize

Even little white lies have a time to shine

The truth will come out

Self congratulatory masturbation

Will only lead to self-contamination

A poisoning of your dream and true self

Until the lines between responsibility and senility

Fade into dementia worn memory

Even sharks smile

Even crocodiles shed tears

And even a sadist can feel pain

-Ivory-

Repetition

Wash

Rinse

Dry

Repeat

These are the ways

To bleach the soul

-Hester-

The Dead whisper epithets, their words, tousled leaves

Hidden in the silhouette of Memory,

the synaptic opium of all our yesterdays have us addicted to all our
tomorrows

Rivers of cigarette smoke flow from the window

And the wind sharpens itself on pine needles along its way to me

Carrying earthy scents

and the heavy musk of the deepening Evening

The dark is a shawl, velvet comfort,

in which to confess the hearts weakness

Undertones layered in the wind and cloud currents shift, a butterfly
flaps its wings

And Death stretches its limbs

Weary

I believe in the truth of slow lightening
The unfolding majesty of the thunderclap
And the promise of Sunrise
I believe in the promise of tomorrow
In the silver-tongued whispers of hope
And the truth of blood and sweat
My sins leaking from my wrists
Eyes bright and heart sound
I denied the dark to embrace the Dawn

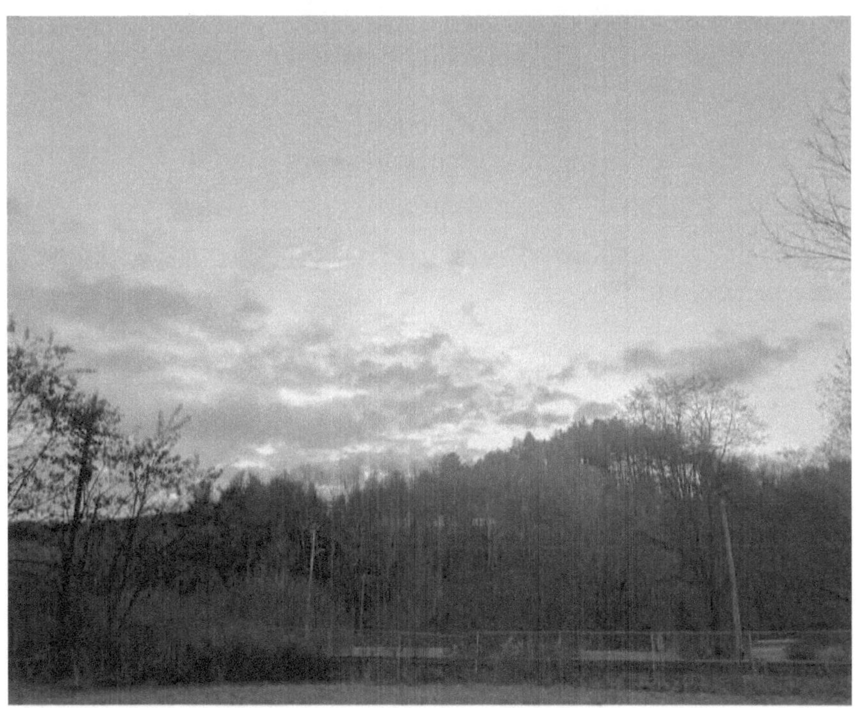

-Endwell-

I'm cucking a cop
His wife is an old high school friend
Who never got to act on her crush
I think I'm starting to love her
And I have a recurring nightmare
He gets shot on duty
Paralyzed from the waist down
And she can never leave
We hang up in silence
And in that silence
I can hear the death of passion
Where does the dream stop
And reality begin?

-The Shining City-

There is a shining city upon the hill

White walled with crimson flags

Seven turrets capped in jade

From it's sturdy ramparts

Golden horns sound their challenge

A roar of lightning rolling over the plains

The Song of Bones is in their blood

There are drums beating behind it's gates

Heads covered in the skins

Of the their enemies

There is a rot within that beauty

A maleficent pulse within a malignant heart

The same hands that crave to build

Also crave to destroy

The same minds that imagine such beauty

Also plot strategies for its end

The same voices that sing songs of joy and love

Also sing songs of sorrow and madness

Songs of blood and broken souls

Songs of a world made undone

And more than any other

They sing the Song of Bones

Of toil and strife made ecstatic

-Diadem-

Dressed in the smoke of memory

Peering through the soot and ash of the past

I am reminded the world cares not

For the anchors of time and memory

The wind blows away all yesterdays

While shadows inhale the pale moonlight

Filtering through the boughs overhead

And the wandering stars trace mystery

A night rain whispers forgotten hymns

Amidst a chorus of thunder

And the accompaniments of lighting

We find sometimes life moves bitterly

The clouds flee East

Revealing the Moon sitting as a diadem

And the stars as gems

Strewn with a careless hand across the nights velvet expanse before
me

My eyes disturb my soul

For the Moon cares not for mortal lives

They garner no notice from the stars above

And always Time is my enemy

Morphean shores beckon near

The tides whisper soft and clear

June is the cruelest month

And sometimes the world is only what we force it to be

All reality is nothing more than the wind through the trees

Hollow whispers in in the dark

Sparks defying nights long memory

All existence a leaf under a burning Autumn Sun

Erupting conflagrations of phantom scarlet and burlesque orange

Tinged with the deeper panic of a yellowing decay we can only delay

Shaken free by the wind through the trees I go now to dream

To embrace sweet slumber And through that dream

Find the Stone Boat within me

-Grey-

I feel hollow

Washed out

Grey and faded white

I'm a ghost

Driving a meat suit

The sidewalk is clear

Except for footsteps of

Frozen snow

It feels like I'm following a memory

An illusion or phantasm

I'm being broken on the Wheel of Time

My mind won't rest

And my heart won't heal

Depression naps prevent restful sleep

And all the rabbit holes are too deep

I chase the early morning silence

Up the sidewalk, anxious and melancholy

A shadow stalking a memory

-Susvórt-

It's so cold it feels like the world will break
The moon a teardrop overhead
Daggers stab deep
Every shuddering I breath I take
A shallow reflection in ice of the world around me
All sharp edges
Translucent, expressionless
A tableau interpreted through frozen eyes
Regret is a cross
The past our Golgotha
It's the sort of cold that fills your soul with glass
When the shakes hit
They're hard enough to snap bone
A Nightingale calls from the trees
The snowfall is heavy
Veðrfölnir sits overhead
Storm pale eyes merciless in their judgement
Huginn and Muninn alight in an Oak
Here to witness and report
My reflection in the ice is not my own
There is no cold
No pain
No weakening limbs
There is only the Sun And peace
I can see it in their eyes

I hear my name upon the wind

The wish to disappear

So completely

As to leave no trace

Not even the whiff of a memory

It grabs me

Deep in my soul

It's claws whisper promises

Of flesh sundered and marrow released

The Spirit free

And unfettered of the mortal coil

Is there surcease in darkness?

Pain forced into anonymity by shadow

Or is it in the light that there's healing?

Even in the palest Winter rays

I chose the light

And the cold

And the pain

Huginn and Muninn alight

Snow falling from their perch

Veðrfölnir turns his gaze

Another wayward soul to judge

The nightingales song echoes across the Dawn

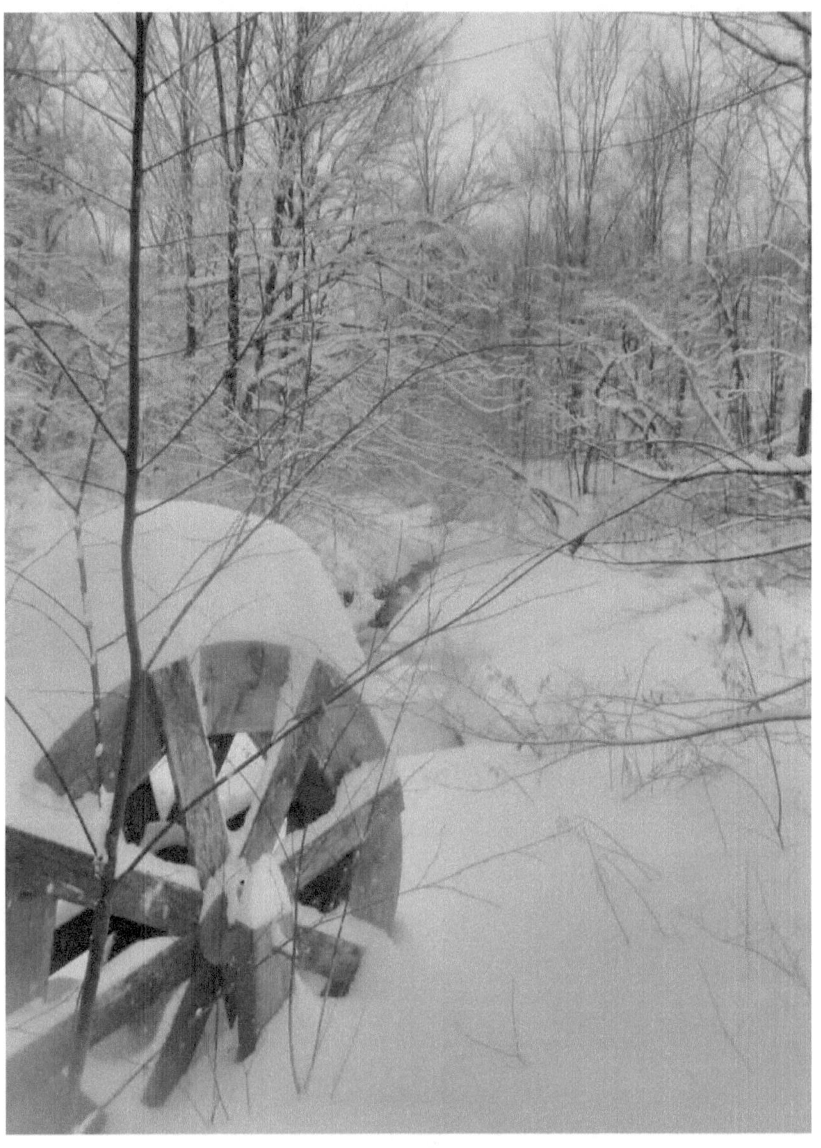

DAYS AND MONTHS

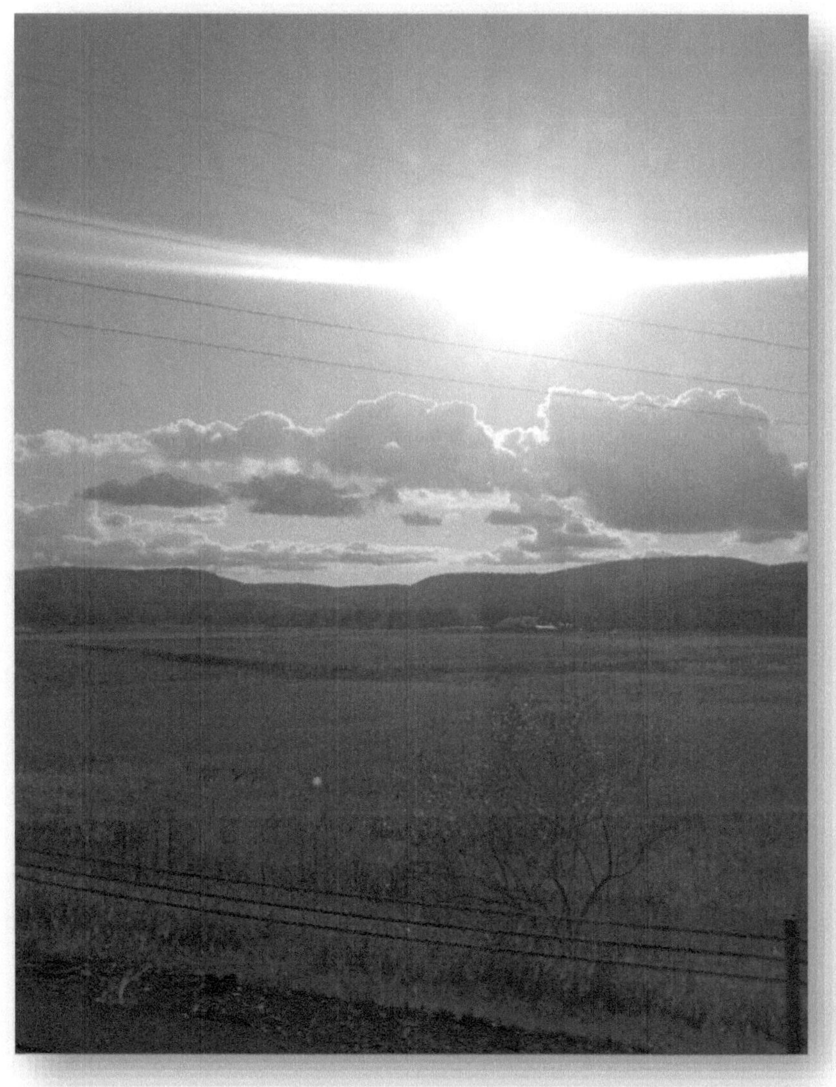

Our lives are made up of seconds, turning into minutes, turning into days, turning to years turning to a life. This section is devoted to days and months that stood out during the course of writing this collection.

This is the eight era.

-Monday-

I don't miss you

To miss is to possess

And I never really had you

You are your soul

But I am alone

That much is certain

A continent apart, adrift

Making my centenary hobble

Millimeters at a time

Seeking foreign shores

With which to collide

I don't feel you

To feel is to touch

And you're gone

You ate the Lotus

I am alone

That much is true

-Tuesday-

'Despair for the future

Surrender to inevitability

Deny hope'

Depression met me at the door

Took me by the hand

And led me to our Wedding bed

Entropy is the womb of Life

The Garden of Ediacra

Holy Chaos its mate

Eyes filled with witch fire

And secret desire

I'm a prisoner in my own soul

Chained to the past

The pain keeps me alive

Electricity in my veins

My reflection doesn't feel real

As if I'm merely a placeholder

For someone else

I am losing my grip on reality

Shadows dance upon the wall

Frantic and gregarious Tuesday

It's just another day

That ends in why?

-Wednesday-

When did the world

Fall apart

The walls fall in

The roof collapse

When did such bitter breezes blow

There is work, unfinished

There are words, left unsaid

There were emotions, unexpressed

And still dreams, left fallow

I'm afraid to breathe

Afraid my slightest

Move may fracture Time

Afraid my sorrow is too shallow

There are no words

No adjectives

No verbs

To explain the desperation I know

One face to the crowd

Brave and optimistic

Never faltering

Never admitting the fear below

Another for the mirror at home

Sad, broken, and alone

My reflection a stranger

Optimism laid low

How do you cradle Atlas?

How do you comfort Prometheus?

You can't give Odin back his eye

And there are some places a soul must go

That the living cannot follow

-Thursday-

Happiness scampers

Across my nerves

Unfamiliar as a new suit

Is that a tingle I feel?

Hello joy

My old friend

How have you been?

What sights

What wonders

Have you brought back to share?

Hope! You old son of a bitch!

Good to see you

God, it's been awhile

Have you met someone?

Will you trade me a secret?

Whisper it in my ear

Me?

I've seen some Sun Seen some rain

But I'm still here

Allowances made for

The passage of Time

I've got some new furrows in my brow

Some new scars, one I can't show

But I'm still here

-Saturday-

A golden late afternoon sunshine Paints the reality I know to be real

A warm embrace I didn't know I needed

The stellar tide provides an air

A breath

A promise of hope in darker times

Go then

Sweet golden rays

Flow then

Sweet summer rains

Embrace my migrant soul and raise me up

Wash the blood from my bones

From my hope

From my dreams

There, by the silver and ochre tinged shore

Tell me my beloved yet lives

Tell me there are still fucks to give

Tell me the past was a sieve Unbind my wings

For I yearn to fly Far from these troubled shores

We've so little time on this Earth

Seconds that slip to menace to slip to tears

And you're wasting them

On equivocation

On verbal masturbation

On the judgement of your peers

-March-

The Sun crept over the horizon

Under a turquoise and charcoal Sky

Spilling like an open vein

Under sullen and indifferent Heavens

The World is an Echo Chamber

Filled with pain

And white noise

Which came first

Crossing your fingers for luck

Or because you were lying?

I think the former

Led to the latter

Because you'd have to be mad

As the Hatter not to see

There is no luck

No destiny

Only pretty lies we tell ourselves

To occlude the cruelty of early Spring

When your love becomes a stranger

Between when they crossed their fingers

And the next

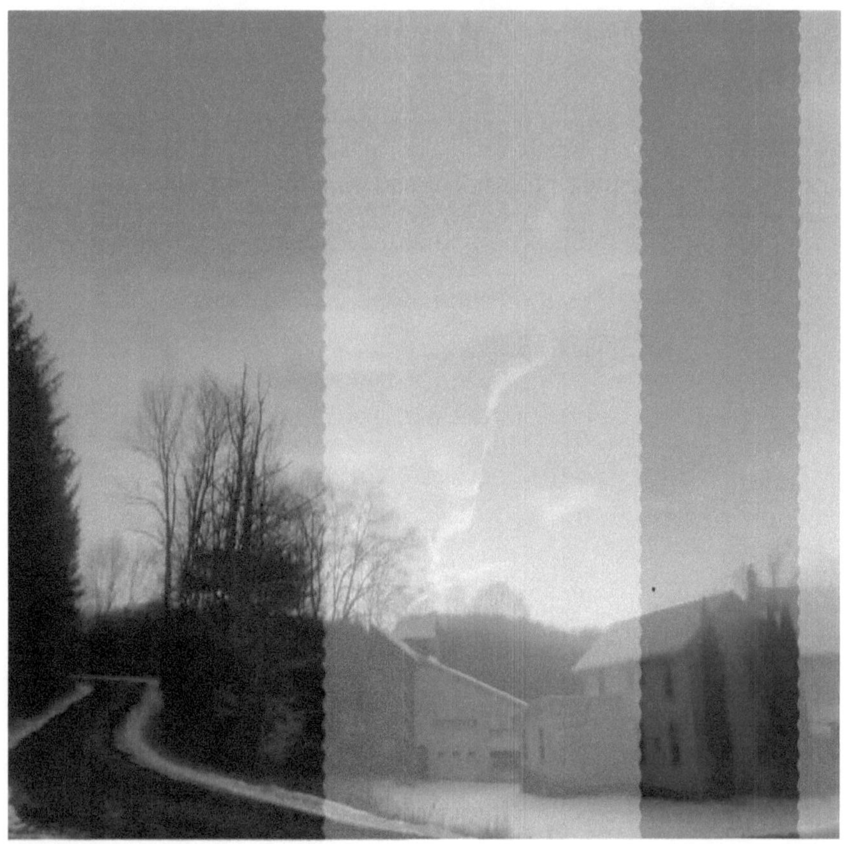

-April-

I want to give you pearls

Diamonds and rubies and sapphires

To anoint thy brow and hang about your

Neck and ears, eternal as my devotion

But you only want space

Like most things when you reach A Certain Age

It's complicated

It's only when we're children things are Simple

I had a dream we sat in my rocking chair

Upon my back porch in the weak

April Sun

The afternoon golden yet muted

The world holding its breath

While Spring peeked shyly about

Uncertain if it's time had come

I traced the circumference of

Your thighs with my fingertips

Marveling at their alabaster sheen

Savoring their silken feel

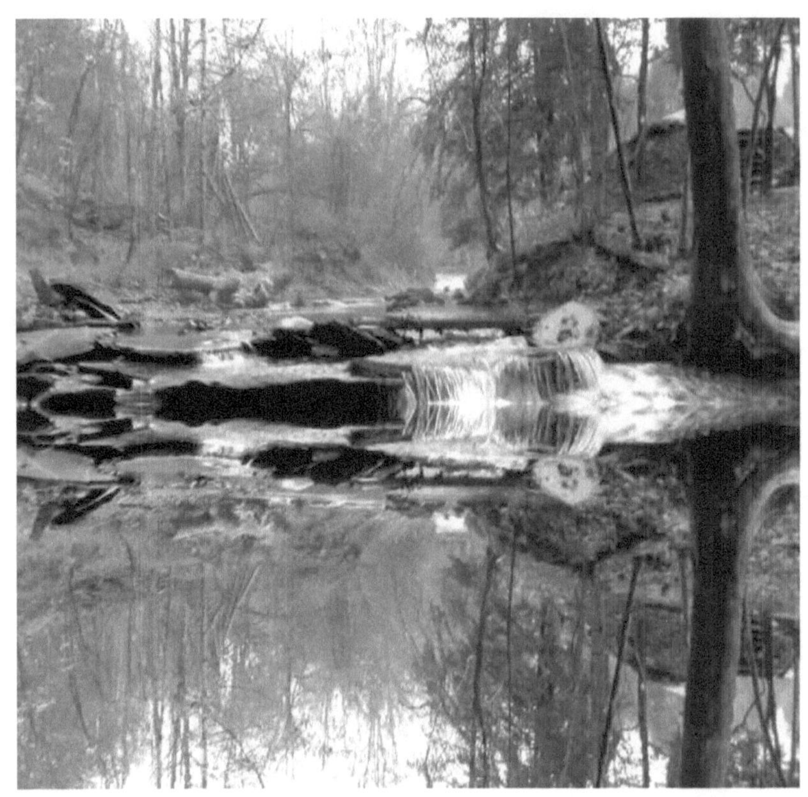

CARA MIA

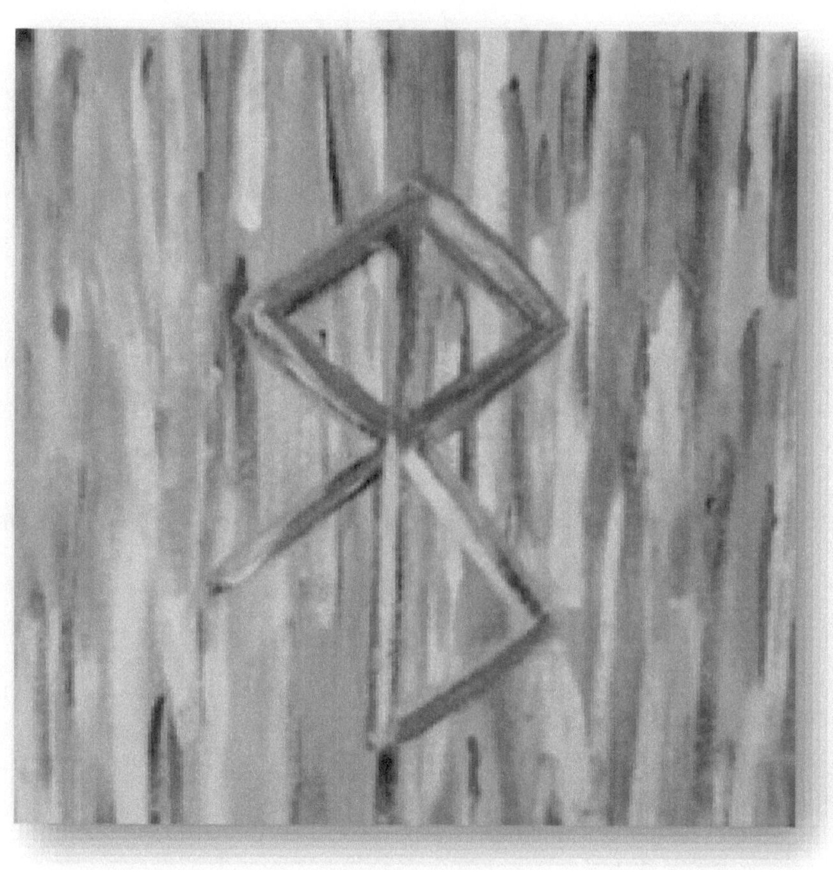

This entire section is dedicated to the love of my life. She knows who she is so I'm not going to embarrass her by calling her out, but none of this would have happened without her love and support.

This is the last era, where I find my life in 2025.

-Cara Mia-

I fell in love with the shattered ghost of yesterday

As I looked for the words I could not say

The voice in the mirror

Couldn't have been any clearer

You're a sorry sight to see, it proclaimed

Afraid to address your fears still unnamed Loneliness

Sadness

Regret

And the son you never met

I shook my head, a denial of the past

Water flew, each droplet a looking glass

Within each was a different me

A facet or choice I could not see

Both Paragon and Pariah

Both Isaac and Iphigenia

The early evening shadows hunted the room

The hard sodium light promising doom

I turned off the faucet

Then went out to smoke a cigarette

I listened to the nights wind song

My thoughts slow and deep and long

The Witching Hour came and went

And still my dark night of the soul wasn't spent

A short rain came and I went out to embrace it

A Baptism and a Gift

I try to follow

My consciousness down the rabbit hole

To drown the chatter of my mind

To quiet the quaver of my soul in kind

Only to find

Golgotha had crept up behind

I contemplated the Moon

And traded secrets with a passing raccoon

There is a darkness in me to which I'll never be immune

A bystander who plots from their tomb

And in the deep of night, they are strong

Their voice carries the night winds song

Though it be right or wrong

Sometimes I have to sing along

Then I remember, she's there, waiting in the Light

And my brain stops it's fright

My heart ceases it's flight

And I remember there is healing in that loves white light

There's redemption in her eyes

And in her arms all pain dies

Together, we are both finally strong enough to ascend to higher skies

And breathe the pure, clean

Air where love never dies

I go back into bed

And beside her I rest my weary head

My eyes grow heavy

I fall into dreams of having finally found the golden thread

That will lead me back home, to the wife

and the family the Universe did intend

-Common Ground-

We sat in the shadow of a maple tree

The stone wall as seats and breaking bread

Searching for truths in what we see

Or for words unsaid

While our eyes still said we'd rather be in bed

Joy, a simple emotion

Fell like the sunshine beyond our shade

Though there was still love and devotion

We slept in the beds we'd made

And paid for it with the love we had made

Apple blossoms as backdrop

Delicate shades of pink and white

Our eyes meet and our hearts stop

And our hearts end the fight

And two become one for one more night

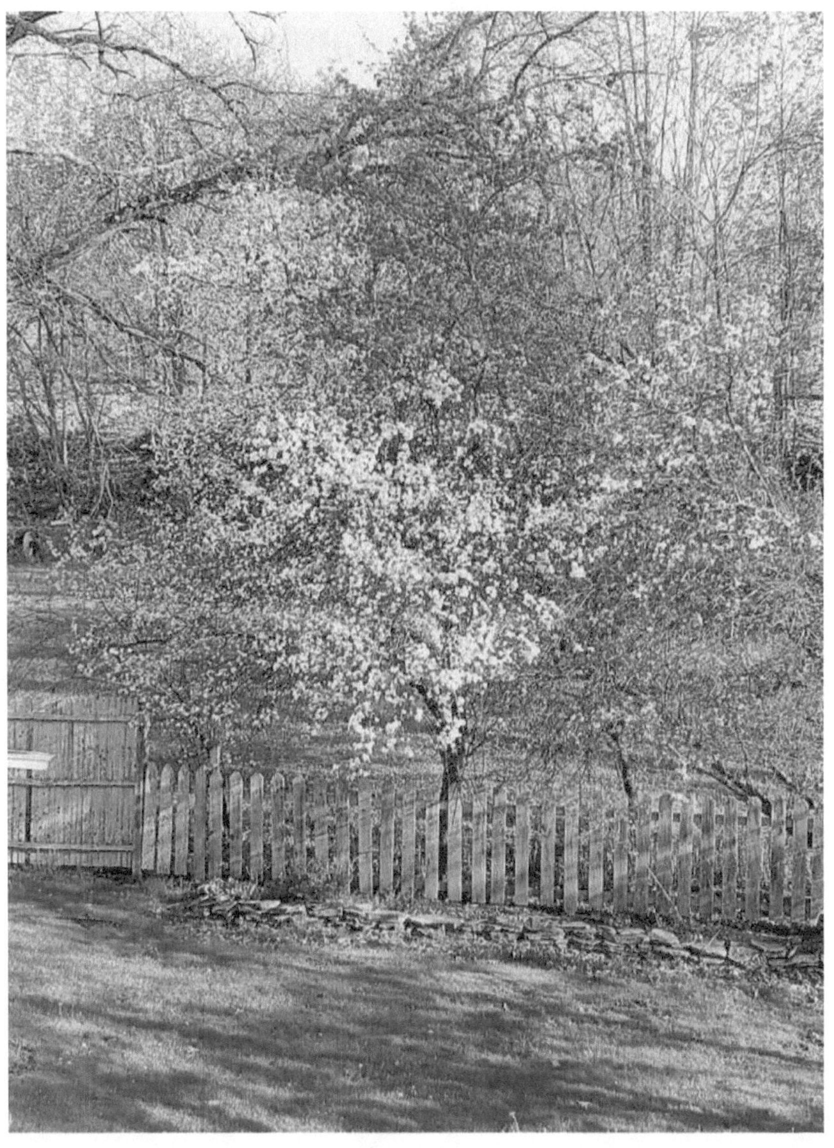

-Another Hand-

Babe

I really did fall in love

I fell in love with you.

No one else

Just you

You give me butterflies when I get one message from you.

I smile secretly when I hear your name because

I feel so lucky to be calling you mine

I love you with all my heart.

-In Dreams-

She came to me in dreams

Wanton and flushed with lustful unvoiced screams

Eager for the kiss that redeems

She said that this was the only place we could meet

To hold each other and let our hearts beat

And where she wasn't the dust beneath his feet I held her close

And gave her a dose

Of our love that always blooms like a rose

When the alarm cried out

I awoke with my ears still filled with her passionate shout

My head cleared of doubt

And I greeted the day

To find that the Dawn held sway

As once again our love had found a way

-Midnight-

The dark is when your heart admits it's fears

All the lost love and the wasted tears

All the broken bones and wasted years

The dark whispers and doubt appears

Winking scarlet dances behind shuttered eyes

A midnight Sun yet to rise

A red handed warning in disguise

Winking scarlet dances, spinning lies

Pearl grey wraps the mind

And speaks of the deceit of time

And the loss of both reason and rhyme

A pearl grey fog denies it's crimes

The dark is when your heart admits its fears

So when the cold hands of doubt appear

So when the soft hands of lies draw near

Never doubt that love was here

-Ghost Stories-

All failed loves are ghost stories

Memories that haunt the waking moments

Shadow plays for a mind caught between dreams

The spectres hiding in our morning coffee

And ghouls stalking our evening meal

Whether they are Hamlet's father

Or a banshee screaming out its loss

All must pay Charon's cost

To ferry the ghost of memory

To night's furthest sea

Whether a wraith lurking near a place of violence

Or a poltergeist raging against its end

They're all whispers against the greater silence

All dreams held tight to the secret heart

You said we're all forgettable

That memory is negotiable

Without trying to start an argument

I'd posit the opposite

We are all part of the Living Memory

All part of a future we can't see

There is no substitute for physical presence

No words that can capture that feeling or essence

After all we've been through

I don't want to become a ghost story to you

-Meridian-

The Summer days pass towards Fall

Pass to funeral pyres, winking against the dark nights shawl

Rumors of distant thunder over the Plains

Gone, gone, gone; wind down empty streets

Passed abandoned cathedrals and empty pews

Burying all under acres of centennial dusts sheets

Piling high into dunes against the façade

Eventually swallowing the sins of a generation

Along with its hopes

Friends pass to acquaintances along meridian dividers

Pass to silhouettes in dreams obscured by waking memory

Friends pass to acquaintances, vampires feeding off each other

Never pausing for the gentler thoughts of yesterday

Or the glory of tomorrow to be unfurled

The hammock swings laconically

Nestled close we speak canonically

Of the depths of our love

And the beauty of the blue sky above

Filtered through leaves of green

There is no truth but the moment

And the moment is love

Dreams of silhouettes or solid memories

You hold the skeleton key to my secret heart

The one I don't give anyone else

So, I lay you down on a bed of moss

To worship at your sacred spring

-The Anchor-

There's an ache inside of me

Whenever we're apart

An emptiness in my life where you're supposed to be

My soul aches, throbbing in remembrance of my missing heart

Under a midnight rain

Lightning bugs danced in winking jade

Darting between the raindrops

The night wind their symphony

The Moon darts behind grey monoliths

Sulking until the morning comes

Peeking over the hilltops

Sun ambles in, it's cheeks flushed

Chasing the shadows from the world

I've got a pocketful of moonbeams

And the remains of my dreams

The tattered ends of second-hand clothes

I feel the pull of Time upon my soul

The bonds of Eternity against my dreams

Ephemeral anchors

Against this physical world

There are no words

Happy, sappy, mad, or sad

I carry the sins of coincidence with me

Anchors against Eternity

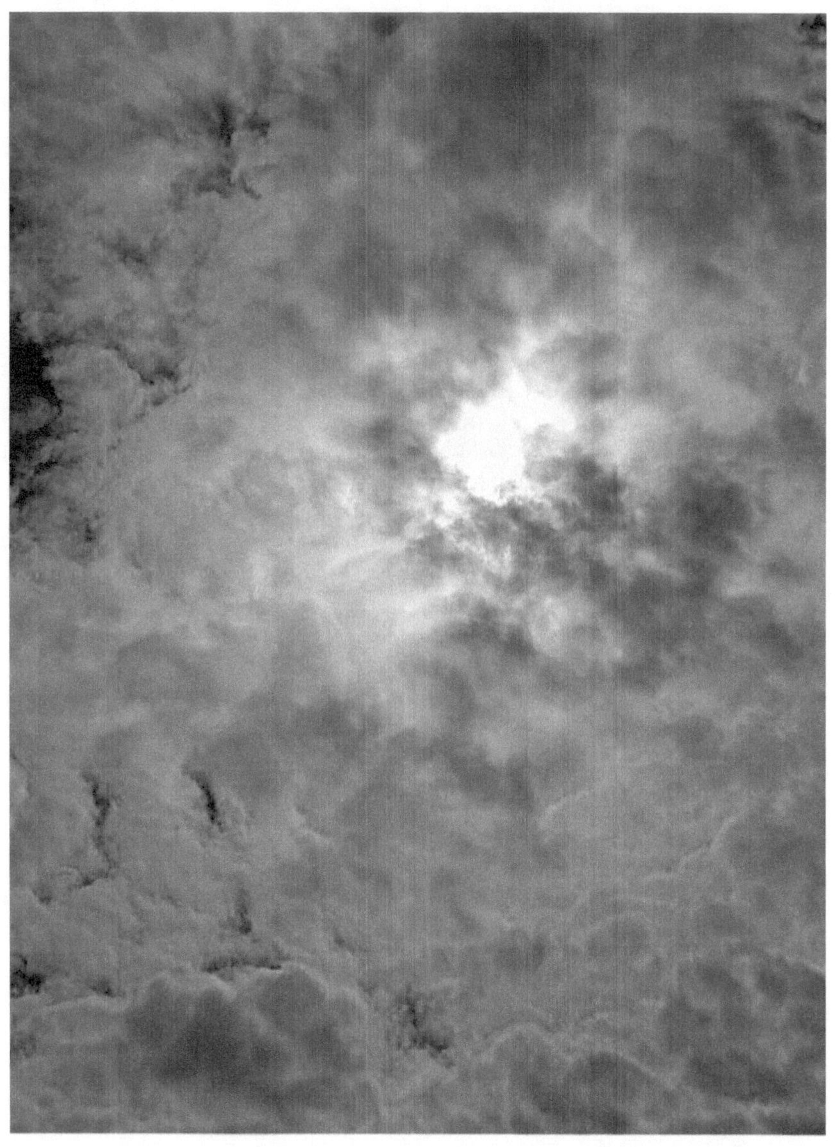

-The Photograph-

The coffee tastes burnt

And my body aches

It's still dark

The moon, it hesitates

While the sun still sleeps

Vindictive and hidden beyond the horizon

Your heart and your soul

Your very bones will ache for me

A vicious pink bloom in the east

For there is no Paradise this side of heaven

That is not found within her arms

I have only a photograph

And this burnt cup of coffee and even though I still hear

Your voice in my ear

And a photograph of us by the beach

On a day the sun hung so low

It seemed within reach

A photograph will never tell you it loves you

It's hair never feels soft under your hands

It's body never warm your own

Never yearn for your embrace

And though it may make your heart race

You'll never know how it's kiss tastes

It's hips will never roll to meet your own

And never find completion within its moan

There's a terrible sadness in photographs

Memory markers for the death of time

Life saturnalia ending in a Barmecidal Feast

I put away the photograph

And finish the coffee

Both are bitter

-Amethyst-

Sweet one

Tell me of your heart

Your dreams and desires

Whisper me an aria

Filled with joy and power

With laughter and hope

Make me immortal with your love

And eternal with your regard

Your words are the song of my soul

-Haty-

Every morning you call my name

Raise me up from my grave

From the clay and the muddy ground

I know there's a ghost

Bleeding all our hope

That we still must lay to rest

I've hewn my words

Syllable by syllable

From the substance of the Stars

Ripped them from the heavens

To place them by your ear

Prayer and crisis in equal measures

I long to talk to you

While holding you close

Nestled in my arms not in my dreams

To feel those ears

Against my lips

To taste your breath

My love for you is encapsulated

Grafted to my DNA

It's in every rain

You are my soul

My heart

My life

My dreams

My gift

My wife

-Under the Gaze of Maple and Crabapple-

A Decembrian fog gathers heavily

In the diamond moons ardent regard

Creeping heavily along an August stalk

In the morning haze

Each breath a steaming, pregnant expectation

Your mercurial ways illum my day with thunderclap embraces

The brooding grey skies could not deny the fire in your eyes

And so we danced

careless as youth in the dawn of the world

To the music of the incoming storms wind

The lightning chased itself among the clouds

But never reached it's fingers toward the ground

And still we danced

Verdant and serpentine, we exalted in the rain

Alive in each other's embrace and holy in each other's eyes

Once the storm had passed

We held each other close and plotted our troth

Under the gaze of the Maple and crabapple

Breathless, our foreheads touching

our thoughts in sync with our hearts and souls

We rushed for the bedroom

Leaving our clothes in a trail behind us on the lawn with careless
abandon

The Dawn breaking over our shoulders

Carry me away, sweet sunrise

Consume me in buxom oranges and a phantom scarlet

In Octoberian hues to frost now dreaming eyes

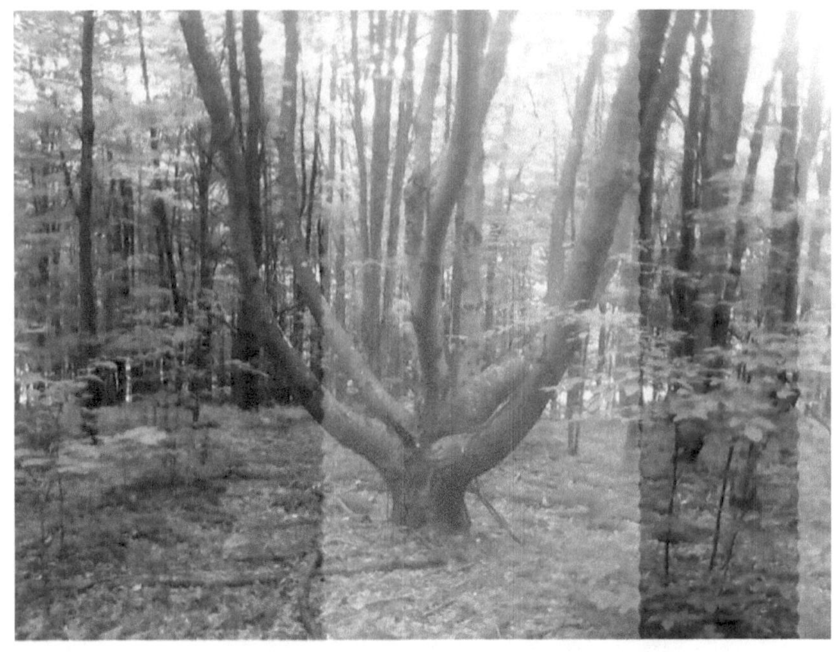

If you made it this far after reading all of that, thank you. My next project is a collection of supernatural short stories set in the river valley of Deposit, New York which will hopefully be out in 2026.

And for that one particular reader, tu es mi corazón Baby Luv, you always will be.